Making
Direct Mail
Work

*Get great results from
all your direct mail*

PETER ARNOLD

How To Books

First published by How To Books Ltd,
3 Newtec Place, Magdalen Road,
Oxford OX4 1RE, United Kingdom.
Tel: (01865) 793806. Fax: (01865) 248780.
email: info@howtobooks.co.uk
http://www.howtobooks.co.uk

British Library Cataloguing in Publication Data.
A catalogue record for this book is available from
the British Library.

Edited by Alison Wilson
Cover design by Shireen Nathoo Design
Cover image by PhotoDisc
Cartoons by Mike Flanagan

Produced for How To Books by Deer Park Productions
Typeset by Kestrel Data, Exeter
Printed and bound by Cromwell Press Ltd, Trowbridge, Wiltshire

NOTE: The material contained in this book is set out in good
faith for general guidance and no liability can be accepted
for loss or expense incurred as a result of relying in particular
circumstances on statements made in the book. Laws and
regulations are complex and liable to change, and readers should
check the current position with the relevant authorities before
making personal arrangements.

THE COLLEGE of West Anglia

TENNYSON AVENUE • KING'S LYNN
TEL: (01553) 761144 EXT 306

LEARNING *Centre*

Contents

Preface

Direct mail. Junk mail. Wastes an awful lot of paper, goes directly into the wastepaper basket and everyone hates it. Right?

Well, no, actually.

Think about it. Would so many large and experienced organisations spend so much time and money on a medium which doesn't give them a return on their investment? Of course not.

Handled properly, direct mail is an extremely powerful marketing tool. For many people it represents a way in which goods and services can be marketed efficiently and profitably. It can be turned on and off as necessary – even at short notice – and above all, its effectiveness can be *measured*.

But note the proviso: 'handled properly'. Much direct mail is wasted because its originators simply don't know what they're doing. It's not good enough to dash off a letter, mail it around the neighbourhood and wait for the business to come in. Direct mail will only work if it is conceived, created and targeted correctly. There's nothing very difficult about it, but you do need to know a few things before you can be confident of success. Once the basic concepts and techniques are understood, there is no reason why any company can't use the medium to great effect.

Large commercial organisations have known this for years, but direct mail is also an ideal tool for the smaller company and for the self-employed person.

Those are the people for whom this book is written. As with everything else in the world of marketing there are virtually no hard and fast rules. Direct mail is not an exact science, although it comes closer to that ideal than any other form of promotion. Anyone can do it. Anyone can profit by it. You'd be hard put to it to find any product or service which can't be sold by it. So direct mail is ideal for the small organisation working on a limited budget.

There are probably as many ideas about direct mail as there are direct mail professionals, some of whom will disagree with some of the things written here. All that can be said on that score is that the book has been written from the standpoint of many years hard-won, hands-on, grass-roots experience, and I make no apologies for that.

One thing I will apologise for, however, is the occasional use of the word 'he' when the context makes it clear that the person concerned could equally well be of the feminine persuasion. There is no intention to be sexist about this: it's done in the cause of writing English which is as readable as possible.

After all, in direct mail, readability is a must.

Peter Arnold

Acknowledgement

Grateful thanks are due to Icon.net Ltd of Barton Street, Gloucester for invaluable help and advice in the preparation of this book.

1

Using Direct Mail

BUILD A BETTER MOUSETRAP . . .

. . . and the world will probably ignore you. Newspapers, magazines, TV, radio, Teletext, the Internet – there are so many media competing for attention these days that the consumer simply has to be selective Otherwise, everyone's brain would become inundated with completely useless information. Yet, somewhere in that avalanche of data are a great many things worth knowing. One of them may be where to acquire a better mousetrap.

As an information provider, someone who has a message to impart, goods or services to bring to the attention of a possible customer, the trick is to evade the built-in filter which consumers have all acquired, and convince them that your message is one worth paying attention to.

But you're probably not the only person out there making better mousetraps. Once you have the attention of your prospective mousetrap buyers, you have to convince them that your better mousetrap is a *better* better mousetrap than the one the other fellow is selling.

Let's take a look at various ways at our disposal of doing that.

USING WORD OF MOUTH

Of course, you can always simply tell people you meet about the goods or services you have to offer. Better still, you can get your satisfied customers to give you a recommendation. There's no doubt that this sort of 'referral', as it is known in the trade, is a very effective way of promoting your business. But it has several crippling disadvantages:

- It's a slow, long-term process.

- You have little control over it.

- It can't be measured effectively.

- You don't know just who is being approached.

- You can't really be sure it is happening at all.

ADVERTISING

Advertising, by which is meant paying good money for a space in a publication or a period of time on radio or TV, is a powerful and effective method of promotion, but it has to be handled with caution.

It was the late Lord Leverhulme who made the most famous comment on advertising. 'I know,' he said, 'that half the money I spend on advertising is wasted. The trouble is, I don't know which half!'

This remark is almost too true to be funny. Any advertisement is seen (but not necessarily noted) by a great many people for whom it has no fascination at all. There is therefore a great deal of wastage involved. For many companies, this doesn't really matter, just as long as the right prospects are influenced. It's a 'shotgun' approach, rather than a 'rifle' one. That's all very well for organisations which can afford a healthy advertising budget, but it does reduce the appeal for small companies or self-employed businesspeople.

Many experts regard advertising as a long-term, 'water on a stone' process – a matter of structured, continuous campaigning. It is, or should be, a highly professional business, involving a whole team of skilled people, working in a whole spectrum of disciplines. This process is frequently not available to many small organisations.

Of course, many ads are inserted in local and other publications by small tradesmen, working off the top of their heads, and some of them undoubtedly work. However, one is entitled to wonder if such a system really does much good. There is no bigger turn-off than a limp, badly designed and written advertisement. Such an animal can actively do harm to an otherwise excellent product.

Think twice before committing yourself

Here are some more thoughts for you:

- Once an ad is placed, you are committed. It may be hard to stop should you want to.

- You could find yourself following up responses which turn out to be useless.

- Measuring effectiveness is difficult.

- Other advertisements compete for the reader's attention.

- You can't choose the company your advertisement keeps.

Organising your public relations

'PR', the generally accepted abbreviation for 'public relations', is the art and practice of getting your information published in the media without actually paying for the privilege. Again, it can be a highly professional process, but it is an art which any reasonably intelligent person can acquire, at least in its simpler form.

PR has several important advantages for the smaller business. To start with, it costs virtually nothing apart from a few postage stamps. Anyone can learn how to write an effective press release in ten minutes, once the rules have been explained.

Any business should run a PR operation. But this is 'as well as' other methods of promotion, and not 'instead of'. There are other aspects to consider, too:

- You are in the hands of journalists, who decide what is actually printed.

- PR is an indirect medium. It isn't intended to stimulate direct sales.

- You can never be sure that your information will actually be published.

- You can't control the readership.

USING OTHER METHODS

There are, of course, several other promotional media you could consider. There is the whole field of **sales promotion**, for example, which covers the spectrum of activities such as competitions, free or money-off offers, free gifts, coupons *etc*. There is also **exhibition** work, **telesales** and **sponsorship**. In most parts of Britain, you can even employ a **town crier**, and very effective he can be, in such areas as **leaflet distribution**, too.

The problem with most of these disciplines is that they don't really stand on their own. They need properly integrated campaigns with advertising or PR support to be really effective. Even telesales are really just a specialised form of direct mail.

Which is where the story really starts.

TAKING ADVANTAGE OF DIRECT MAIL FLEXIBILITY

Direct mail probably has as much potential for improving your business as any medium, except perhaps for television advertising, which is expensive. It also has more pitfalls than any medium, except for television, so you must do the job properly, and eliminate all the common errors which companies who simply 'dash off a letter' are prone to commit. So let's take a look at what direct mail can offer you.

To begin with, direct mail is the most flexible medium you will find. It can be used to sell goods and services including everything from consumer items through products for commerce and industry, to highly technical materials and equipment for the scientific community. It can also be very effective for charities and other fund-raising organisations.

There are even areas where a good direct mail letter is preferable to any other sort of approach: certain aids to health come into this category, for example. We all have areas of our lives which we don't particularly want everyone to know about.

But there is more to direct mail flexibility than its universal applicability:

- You can target your specific market very accurately.

- You can set your own geographical parameters.

- You can identify new, and sometimes unexpected, markets.

- You can 'turn direct mail on and off' at very short notice.

- You can vary your offer depending on the company or individual you are approaching.

- You can initiate a new campaign very quickly, if an opportunity arises.

And that's probably only a partial list. You'll probably think of other examples of direct mail flexibility as this book progresses.

MEASURING EFFECTIVENESS

Another great advantage of direct mail is that you can measure how effective your operation is, and you can do it continuously. You know how many reponses you get from any given mailing, and can take advantage of the successful ones, and modify the ones which don't seem to be doing so much good.

No other medium can be measured quite so exactly, which is why so many companies spend so much money on opinion polls to find out how effective their advertising is.

This measurability has important implications:

- You will find that some days of the week are more suitable for mailing than others.

- You will be able to get a fair knowledge of just how seasonal your product is.

- You will be able to refine your prospect list continuously.

- You can even judge how the weather affects response!

TAILORING YOUR AUDIENCE

You will have a fair idea before you start of the sort of individual or company most likely to take advantage of your product or service. But a well-structured direct mail campaign will give you a great deal more useful information. Many a company has modified its packaging, or even the product itself, as a result of information gathered through its direct mail.

One very large multi-national organisation found, for example, that there was an unexpected market for one of its photocopiers in the farming community. So it changed the name of that particular product, and packaged some of its output of that model specifically for agricultural use.

GETTING THE TIMING RIGHT

It's a fairly unusual business which has a steady flow of work coming in throughout the year. Almost everyone has peaks and troughs, if only in the busy period before Christmas, and the doldrum month or so afterwards.

But you might be surprised. You may be able to use direct mail to improve your business during the slow periods and, of course, you could use it to maximise your profitability at times you know to be potentially fruitful.

You might even find areas – geographic or demographic – where there is an unexpected demand during your traditionally slow periods.

One sophisticated Midlands-based telephone answering service used a small direct mail shot to find new customers who needed telephone cover over the Christmas period. The company then found that it retained a significant proportion of the new business because the new clients avoided the necessity to take on more staff in the slow New Year period. A very nice surprise indeed, and one which the telephone service would not have thought of without their initial mailing.

ENSURING COST EFFECTIVENESS

One of direct mail's great advantages is that you can control your budget very accurately. If you find that your campaign isn't working, then you simply stop it. Or you can extend it if the converse is true.

But there are extensions to this advantage. You can:

- easily calculate how much each individual mailer is costing you
- just as easily discover how much each *response* has cost you
- then, by keeping accurate records of the source of each completed sale, work out how much each eventual piece of business has cost.

You'll find that this is a great advantage in doing your annual budgeting. If you can predict, with some degree of accuracy, how much you will spend on acquiring business, then you are ahead of the game. And your bank manager will certainly approve!

CHECKLIST

Here's a list of things you should know before you can start to plan an efficient direct mail campaign.

What are your geographical parameters?
List towns and villages, suburbs *etc* which you can service economically.

Who is your potential market?
Do you want to reach

- Companies?

- Large companies or small?

- Other organisations, *eg* local authorities, voluntary sector, charities?

- Self-employed people?

- Families?

- Individuals?

- If so, what is the likely age range?

- Male, female or both?

- Householders?

- Approximate income levels?

- Anyone else?

How much do you want to spend?
That's a tricky one for someone inexperienced in such matters. A good rule of thumb is to take a figure of between two and four per cent of your anticipated annual turnover. This will give you a figure which you can look at and perhaps say 'You must be joking!' or maybe 'Oh. I can afford a bit more than that!'

This isn't graven in letters of stone, and doesn't work for every type of business, but in lieu of any other parameter it will serve. And it does, at least, give you a direct mail budget somehow rooted in your business, which is far preferable to plucking a figure out of the air.

CASE STUDIES

Phil hopes to reach his audience more efficiently

Phil runs a small home maintenance service. He only employs a couple of men, plus a secretary, relying on employing craftspeople and casual labour to fulfil many of his contracts.

He likes the idea of using direct mail because it offers him a way to reach his potential market without spending a lot of money on advertising, which he has found to be 'spotty' in its effectiveness from his point of view. He can also see opportunities to refine his market, and to be able to know, some time in advance, when he is likely to have to employ his band of freelance labour.

Howard wants to use his salesmen more effectively

Howard owns a small company selling stationery and office equipment. He has a couple of salesmen and a small office staff. Direct mail is attractive to him because it can cut the amount of cold calling his reps will be asked to undertake. He also hopes to reach new customers in the commercial field and, just as important, the individuals within those companies who have buying influence. He can see that the opportunity to send businesslike letters to selected executives will improve the image of his company in the business community.

Lynn needs to reach new people

Lynn is a fundraiser for a sizeable charity. She needs to increase donations, and to find extra voluntary helpers. She can see that properly constructed direct mail can be a very controllable and cost-effective way of achieving both ends. It certainly has advantages over charging around her wide geographical area, running up petrol and car maintenance bills. Direct mail also offers Lynn a way to reach new sections of the business and charity-supporting community, opening up her fields of operation in a structured and controllable way.

2

Deciding What to Do

DEFINING WHO YOU ARE

It's difficult to get from A to B unless you know where you are in the first place. So you can't expect to do an effective job of promoting your products or services unless you have a shrewd idea of where you stand in your chosen marketplace.

But before we start to find out, a word or two of advice.

First, this is no time to be modest. You are, of course, the best in the world at what you do. You would have no hesitation in recommending your enterprise to anyone who wants to use it. At least, that's the standpoint you take from the beginning, but you must define your terms in order to justify that statement.

Defining your competitors

Very few businesses have a monopoly situation. Almost everyone has competitors of some sort. Even if you are the only one supplying your service in your area, you must ask yourself, 'How did people cope before we arrived?' You will then find that people *were* able to get by, and that your job is to persuade them that you are offering something new and different.

For example, one group of enthusiasts opened a cyber café in a West Country city which didn't have one. With high hopes and enormous confidence, they opened their doors and waited for the crowds to roll in. And of course – they didn't.

Why not? They were, after all, offering something completely new in their area, something fashionable, new and exciting. People ought to be battering their doors down to get in.

Life, unfortunately, is not like that. Further consideration revealed that most people who were interested in exloring the Internet were very happy to use their own PCs at home. Others, who might have been interested, were, frankly, a little bit frightened of the whole business. There were also people who wanted to become Internet users, but who were unwilling to make the initial investment involved before they had tested the water, so to speak.

This last group was a useful nucleus of customers, but they were complete beginners, and needed a certain level of training before they could use the facilities offered with any degree of confidence, which was time consuming and not very profitable. When they did become proficient, they bought their own systems and disappeared from the scene.

It was at this point that the organisers realised that they *did* have comptition, and who it was. It turned out to be the cafés, pubs, clubs and other places of entertainment. A simple change of emphasis in terms of the refreshments provided, and the general ambience of the establishment, changed things completely and, over a period, trade built up very satisfactorily, aided by a PR operation in the local press.

Assessing the competition

Whoever you are, you do have competition of some sort, and although you have enormous confidence in what you're offering, you have competitors who can provide some aspects of your service better than you can.

- Do you have direct competition: rivals who are offering exactly the same services as you are?

- Do some of them have more experience at the job than you?

- Do some of them have a price advantage over you, perhaps because they can buy in bulk, or have fewer overheads?

- Do some of them offer a more high-quality service than yours?

In fact, taking price and quality into consideration, just where are you in the marketplace?

- Are you offering top-of-the-range service, in terms of quality, workmanship or craftsmanship, and charging a premium price for doing so?

- Are you offering a first-rate middle-of-the-range job at a fair price for a fair service?

- Are you, frankly, cheap and cheerful? Offering a popular product, probably in quantity, to customers who don't want to spend too much money?

There's nothing wrong with any of these sectors of the market. But you'd better be sure which one you fall into.

There are, of course, other questions to ask yourself, too. Do you have a geographical limitation? Are some jobs too large or small for you to undertake economically? Do you intend to work 'office hours' or can you offer a 365-day, 24-hour service?

You may well think of other parameters you should set yourself, but, in the end, you are the best in the world at what you do *within those parameters*.

IDENTIFYING YOUR PROSPECT

So now you have a fair idea where you stand. So how about your **prospects** – the people or organisations you would wish to influence?

- Are you going to mail to individuals in their private or their business capacity?

- So – are you writing to them at home or at work?

- Do you therefore need lists of home addresses or businesses?

- Are your prospects likely to be male, female, either or both?

- Is there likely to be an appropriate age range (*eg* teenagers or the elderly)?

- How much are you asking your prospect to spend (substantial investment or 'pocket money')?

- Are you approaching prospects locally, regionally or nationally?

No one knows your business as well as you do, so the above list of questions may not be exhaustive in your case. But you get the idea: by answering those questions, and perhaps some others you'll regard as appropriate to your own situation, you will be able to build up a profile of your likely, average, prospect.

It's worth stressing that word 'average' because sometimes there can be surprises. One nationally known office equipment supplier never did work out why one particular product range received an unexpectedly high response from wholesale jewellers! Not even the *jewellers* could tell them. It was just one of those statistical quirks which can arise from time to time. In the end, the company just accepted the business gratefully, and carried on mailing to that particular list.

The reverse can also be true of course. Occasionally, you will find a group of people, apparently stone-cold certainties in terms of a good response, who seem to treat your offer with supreme indifference.

In spite of the story above, however, a little bit of digging, and asking around, can usually reveal why such anomalies occur. And that's another piece of useful information tucked away in your files.

ESTABLISHING FREQUENCY

Very few businesses have a nice, steady flow of work. Life would be much easier if they did, but most people find themselves handling peaks and troughs in their activities, and these are often predictable. For some organisations, for example, the traditional July–August holiday season is a relatively dead one, while for others, the advent of the school holidays causes a flurry of activity.

Your knowledge of such patterns can be used to decide *when* you run a mailing campaign, and also *how often*.

When considering a direct mail operation, there are quite a few factors which might influence your decision on when and how often to mail. Here are a few. You may well think of others.

- Can you foresee a seasonal variation? Christmas? School holidays? Others?

- How much time can you afford to spend on running your campaign? Do you have enough help back in your office? Can you spend much time on the operation yourself, or should you be out in the field?

- How much time will it take you to act on the returns you get from your mailing? Will it be simply a matter of posting off literature, or should each response entail a personal visit or contact? You might not want to send off another batch of mailers while your existing replies are building up.

- Are there geographical considerations? Do you want to cover a particular area – say a neighbouring suburb – before moving on elsewhere, or should you be mailing over your whole geographical field of operations at the same time, perhaps to keep your sales force busy?

- How do you see your operation developing? Should you be taking a continuous 'water on a stone' approach, or are you contemplating a periodic 'blitz' on appropriate prospects in specific areas?

- There is, of course, always the budget to consider. When you've done all your homework, how many times can you afford to mail?

But please – don't decide to 'try one and see how it goes'. It won't tell you anything. If your test mailing is successful, then you could be enthused into plunging ahead into a costly campaign on the basis of far too little information. If it fails, you'll never be sure just why nothing much happened, and you could throw the whole concept out prematurely. A 'so-so' response will leave you just as ill-informed as you were in the first place.

Much better to test the water by means of a carefully structured, albeit fairly modest, campaign, geared to give you as much information as it can.

MAKING AN OFFER

So just what are you going to offer your prospect? Obviously you want him to take advantage of your products or services, but what **initial response** do you wish your mailing to provoke?

You could be trying to persuade potential customers to visit your store or showroom, in which case you could enclose a money-off coupon, invite the reader to a special demonstration, offer a limited-period discount . . . You know your business best. You'll think of something.

Perhaps you will be offering an informative piece of literature. For example, a travel agent might wish to supply a brochure detailing holidays available. If you're supplying capital equipment to business or industry, then you will want your prospect to read full details of your product, in which case, again, the right informative brochure can be very attractive to an appropriate company buyer.

You could simply be on a list-building exercise, hoping to derive a database for future sales efforts. Charities, for example, can benefit from this sort of approach, providing themselves with lists of people who have sympathies with their particular causes. In that sort of case, an appropriate free gift offer can be effective.

The point is that there could well be an intermediate stage between your prospect reading your mailing, and you persuading him to avail himself of your products and services. That stage can often be covered by a visit from a representative, in which case your rep will need some reason to follow up the response. 'Did you find our brochure informative, sir?', 'Is there anything further I can do for you?', 'When can I come and see you?'

Make up your mind quite quickly just what reaction you want from your prospect, and then think about the best way to stimulate it.

SETTING A BUDGET

Deciding how much money you are going to spend on your mailing operation depends on a whole variety of factors. Some of them can be considered here, and some of them can't because they have to do with your company's financial structure, available resources and administration. For example, just when does a mailing expense stop being a mailing expense and become a charge on your overall sales budget? Sending out a follow-up brochure should probably be charged to the mailing campaign, but a follow-up visit from a rep probably shouldn't. Only your financial wizards and yourself can define those parameters.

However, by taking into account all the topics discussed in this chapter, you should be able to get a fair idea of how much you should be spending on your direct mail operation. You'll now be able to estimate:

- how many mailing operations you envisage in the period in question

- how many actual mailers you will be sending out during the course of those mailings

- therefore, how much the postage will cost (but consult the Post Office: they may be able to minimise that cost for you)

- how expensive your mailed material is likely to be, *ie* print costs *etc*

- what your follow-up costs will be.

There is a rule of thumb which can be applied. It states that if you look at your company's estimated turnover for the financial year in question, then a figure of around four per cent of that is an appropriate one to spend on all forms of promotion. It is just a 'rule of thumb', however, and doesn't apply to all businesses by any means. Nevertheless, it does give you a figure which is related to your business, and isn't simply plucked out of the air.

Having derived that figure you can look at it and think 'Wha-at! You must be joking!' or 'Oh! I don't know. I can afford a bit more than that.' At least, it's somewhere to start.

There is a refinement used by rather larger and long-established organisations, perhaps when they're contemplating the launch of a new product. They can take the turnover figure for the next *three* years in that particular sector of the business. They then take a percentage of that, and spend half of that figure in the first year, and the other half in the following two years. The point being, as one wise old lecturer on the subject used to say, 'You don't pull the trigger quietly!'

Remember, that figure, whatever it turns out to be, covers *all* promotional work and not just direct mail. If you are running an advertising campaign at the same time – and it's often to be recommended that you do – then those costs have to come from the same figure.

The important thing is that you do establish a budget and stick to it. It's fatally easy to be open-ended about things, especially if your mailings are proving successful, but it's a great way to run away with a lot of money without even realising it.

DECIDING YOUR 'TONE OF VOICE'

Having considered all the factors above – where you fit into your marketplace, who your best prospects are likely to be, how often and just when you are likely to mail, and approximately how much you intend to spend on each piece of mailing material – you can start thinking about **what form** your mailers will take.

- Will you be producing glossy, high-quality mailers?

- Or is a strictly business-letter approach more appropriate for your market?

- Are you going to be highly selective in your choice of recipients (in which case the unit cost of each mailer can be comparatively high)?

- Or are you going to mail a large number of pieces to a wider audience (in which case you may have to spend less on each recipient)?

- How are you goiong to 'speak' to your prospect? In strictly businesslike terms, or in a more informal 'tone of voice'?

- Do you foresee a need for illustration, which is comparatively expensive?

- Or can you get by with simple words in a letter format?

- Should you be producing a special letterhead for your mailings?

- Will you be producing another piece of literature for follow-up purposes?

Now you should have enough information to decide just how you're going to tackle the whole process of running a mailing campaign.

CHECKLIST

Define yourself: are you:
- a market leader
- a newcomer to the field
- well known in your particular marketplace?

Who is your competition?
- existing businesses in the same market
- companies in similar but different trades
- don't know.

Who are your best prospects?
- existing customers
- individuals at home
- businesses
- men
- women
- both
- children and their parents

- householders
- the elderly and retired people
- others.

Where are they geographically?
- national
- regional (define)
- local (define).

Frequency: are you going to mail:
- regularly (weekly, monthly, whatever)
- seasonally (holidays, Christmas, winter, spring, summer, autumn *etc*)
- an occasional 'blitz'
- for special purposes (new products, spring lines, *etc*)?

Will you be offering:
- follow-up literature
- a rep's visit
- a discount
- 'money-off' offers
- a free gift
- a free estimate
- a demonstration
- other?

Your budget
- What is the total sum available for mailing over the period in question?
- How many mailings do you envisage over that period?
- Therefore, you can spend £ . . . per mailing.
- How many mailers do you intend to send out for each mailing?
- Therefore, you can spend £ . . . per mailer (including postage *etc*).
- Look at your other costs:
    postage
    packing
    fulfilment (*ie* follow-up costs)
    other.

(*NOTE: these are only approximate costings so that you can see which 'ball park' you are in. They can be revised and refined as the process continues, or circumstances change.*)

'Tone of voice': are your mailers to be:
- glossy, high quality
- 'jazzy' with plenty of illustration *etc*
- businesslike
- 'cheap and cheerful'?

CASE STUDIES

Phil decides to be selective
Phil has decided to identify three or four localities, within reasonable reach of his base, which consist mainly of older properties which would benefit from his maintenance and building services. He intends to run a blanket mailing of all of them.

Phil's idea is to mail each locality in rotation, aiming at one mailer per household about every three or four months, but is prepared to modify that system as events transpire. Hopefully, he will have to stop his mailings occasionally, because he will have quite enough work on hand.

His budget won't let him use expensive mailers, so he intends to produce attractive, but inexpensive letters, and will offer a free estimate to people who respond.

Howard pulls out all the stops
Howard knows he has a new product range to launch, and wants to give his small sales force every chance to operate effectively. He has decided to mail all his existing customers – always his best prospects – plus a prospect database he has built up over a long period. In addition, he will be seeking to mail as many company administration officers as he can locate within a radius of around 50 miles.

His approach will be businesslike, using a signed letter and reply card. His offer will be a brochure supplied by the manufacturer of the product in question, plus a free demonstration on the prospect's own premises. However, his reps will be instructed to follow up all leads received from the mailing.

Lynn decides on her offer
Lynn is seeking new members for her wildlife charity. She has decided to mail over a wide area, depending on how far her budget will stretch: if it all works well, she may 'go national'.

She believes her mailings need illustration, but does not want to go so upmarket that prospective members may consider she is wasting the charity's money. Nevertheless, she can foresee that her mailings will be comparatively expensive, which will restrict the number she can send out.

She will offer a free copy of her charity's attractive newsletter, plus reduced-price one-year's subscription for new members.

3

Tailoring Your Campaign

Having gone through the various processes outlined in the previous chapter, you should have a fair idea where you want to go from here. You'll know where you fit into the marketplace, who are likely to be your best prospects, how intensive your campaign is likely to be, and how much money you are prepared to spend. That's fine. Now you're ready for the next step, which is refining and firming up on your course of action.

You could say that the last chapter was strategy, and this one is *tactics*.

DECIDING YOUR MARKET

Now you know who your best prospects are, you can take a closer look at them. You may, for example, have a budgetary restraint which prevents you approaching all of them, in which case you'll need to decide who are your *best* best prospects.

Business versus private individual

Here's where selling by direct mail to the business community tends to part company with marketing to the individual. A man sitting behind his desk, spending his employers' money, may well be a much harder nut to crack than *exactly the same individual* sitting at home with a certain amount of disposable income which he may be prepared to apply to your goods or services.

A chap sitting at home, in a T-shirt, opening his post over a cup of coffee may well be vulnerable to a spot of impulse buying, for example. Once he puts on his jacket and tie, and has his post brought to him by his secretary, such flashes of liberality probably don't happen. After all, if he makes a wrong decision in his private capacity he can write the whole thing off to experience, and receive nothing worse than the disapproval of his wife and family. A similar incorrect decision at work could, in theory anyway, lose him his job.

There are different sets of prejudices, too. In his or her private capacity, an individual might have decided not to buy products originating in a country of whose government or human rights record he disapproves. Company executives don't usually have that luxury. The products they buy are probably selected purely on fitness for purpose, value for money and similar commercial considerations.

In some ways a commercial or industrial customer is more easily defined than is a private prospect. In the first case, he is more likely to fit into a well-known stereotype. The individual has an enormous baggage of quirks, foibles, prejudices and preferences.

Not that the business executive doesn't have those things too. He just can't indulge them so much.

So how does that sort of consideration affect your direct mail campaign?

Quite simple. You can't approach a business customer in the same way as you would an individual consumer.

But please remember. In both cases you are, in the initial stages anyway, dealing with individuals. Even if you are selling to a large, hard-nosed business organisation, if you can't impress the first person to read your letter, then your whole operation stops right there.

So let's start with the easier option: the industrial or commercial prospect.

MAILING TO INDUSTRY AND COMMERCE

It's all very well mailing to a business concern, but just who do you approach within that company? You obviously need a name (preferably) or a job title if your mailer is going to get any further than the receptionist's wastepaper basket. The question you have to ask yourself is:

- **Who makes the buying decision?**

Not always an easy one to answer. Who decides to buy which product isn't always the same person as the one who is going to use it. You wouldn't try to sell floor polish to the office cleaner, would you?

The problem of finding the right decision-maker escalates with the size of the company concerned. There's no difficulty with self-employed people and small operations, but medium-sized companies probably present you with a range of options, and in very large organisations there can be over 100 people involved in the buying process.

Building your mailing list

If you've been in business for a while, you'll already have a start. You have a client or customer list, and don't forget that you have a list of suppliers too. You may be a member of a Chamber of Commerce, a trade association, a professional body or similar organisation. And don't be shy about using names of social contacts, either. A list of Rotary members, for example, can yield some very useful prospects.

However, you'll probably find that the bulk of your mailing list will be made up of people addressed by their job titles rather than by name, and there could be several such titles which are grist to your mill. You'll have to decide which of them are likely to yield the best results.

Remember, one of the advantages of direct mail is the ability to test this sort of thing. Over a series of mailings you can find out which job title gives you the best return on your mailing investment.

All this assumes that you intend to build your own mailing list. There are, of course, alternatives. Direct mail agencies in your area will be delighted to do your mailing for you, to a high professional standard, to lists provided by them. But it's an extra expense, of course.

MAILING TO INDIVIDUALS

One can assume that people making buying decisions in a professional capacity do so for thoroughly professional reasons. Is the product under consideration the best for the job? Is there a price advantage? – and so on. You can't make the same assumption when dealing with an individual, sitting at home with no one to second-guess him, except perhaps his family. All his preferences and prejudices are given full rein.

This means that one has to be more careful how you speak to him. After all, you are, quite literally, hitting him where he lives. The whole thing becomes much more personal, and your mailer can end up in the waste basket through no fault of your product or service, but purely because you have given him some, quite illogical, reason to dislike you. 'There's nowt so queer as folk', as the old North Country saying goes, and you ignore that fact at your peril.

The converse is that he might equally well decide to return your reply card for similarly illogical reasons. Something in your mailer may have appealed to him – or her – and created a desire to know more about your product, probably on impulse.

All this means that you do need to know a great deal about your potential customer if you are to have any chance of influencing him to take the matter further. Luckily, you probably know a lot already. Take a look at the list below, and tick off the categories which apply in your case. If you don't know, then do your homework and find out.

Which of the following is likely to apply to your customer?

(Please note: this is not necessarily an either/or situation. Your customers could be both male and female, for example. If that's so, then tick both.)

Male	Managerial
Female	Clerical
Young	Manual
Middle-aged	Foreign holidays
Elderly	UK holidays
Fit	No holidays
Energetic	Sociable
Sedentary	Retiring/quiet
Car driver	Community-minded
Householder	Insular
Mortgagee	Fashion conscious
Tenant	

You may well think of other categories which fit your particular circumstances. If so – well, you get the idea. What you need to do is build a profile of the person who is most likely to take advantage of your offer. But don't be too restrictive about it. The rule should be 'if in doubt – mail them'.

LOCATING YOUR PROSPECTS

So now you now who you might, with advantage, send your mailers to. The problem now is to find them.

If your prospects come from the business or industrial community, then there isn't too much difficulty. Such establishments don't tend to move house as often as individuals and families do, so such reference sources as *Yellow Pages*, telephone directories and trade publications should be reasonably up to date In addition, bodies such as Chambers of Trade and Commerce and professional organisations often make their member lists available, although there may be a fee to pay.

You may feel that you can locate your business customers reasonably accurately in the known commercial and industrial areas of the locality in question. But don't forget that there can be large numbers of 'non-conforming' businesses, located in the most innocuous looking residential streets. Examples would be ladies running secretarial agencies from their homes, self-employed builders and the like.

Mailing to individuals at home presents a completely different set of problems, and this is where your profile of your best prospects comes into play. For example, you may have decided that your interests are best served by approaching middle-aged, middle-management householders with a mortgage. That immediately gives you a fair picture of the type of property he or she is likely to live in.

Your knowledge of your local area will give you appropriate neighbourhoods, estates or whatever for your purposes. If you intend to mail to an area which is new to you, then a couple of drives around the localities in question can give you a great deal of information in a very short time.

DEFINING THE GEOGRAPHY

You now have a good idea about where you are going to send your mailings. But there may be a pitfall you should take into account, and this concerns how you intend to follow up your responses once they start to come in.

There's no point in achieving a response which won't be profitable for you because of the difficulty of reaching some off-the-beaten-track spot. Conversely, you wouldn't want to miss out on useful business just because the prospect concerned happens to be based a few yards on the wrong side of an arbitrary line on a map. Simply sticking a compass point on your base and drawing a neat circle around the area you intend to cover isn't really good enough.

By all means, take your map and draw your neat circle. Then take a closer look. Business premises tend to congregate in specific areas, or sprawl along major roads. Residential properties of a specific type or value are inclined to be found on estates or along roads built at around the same time.

It is therefore worth while tracing lines around or along areas which may be useful to you. You'll probably end up with a shape which looks like a hyperactive octopus, but you will have defined a selling area which offers you maximum chance of success.

USING YOUR BUDGET EFFECTIVELY

At this point you'll be beginning to see a pattern. You'll have a fair idea of your intended target area and the size of the potential market it offers you. You'll know a lot about your prospective customers and will be deciding how best to approach them. You will probably even be getting ideas about what to say in your mailings and how to say it.

You'll also be starting to get **enthusiastic**. So it's as well to pull yourself up sharply and temper your eagerness to get started with reality. In other words – take a look at your budget. You know what you'd like to do, but are you sure you can afford it?

Deciding what you *can* afford

One useful exercise is to estimate the number of prospects you have in your chosen area. It doesn't have to be accurate at this point, just a 'ball park' figure will do. Then do a simple division sum and estimate how much you can afford to spend on each potential customer. The answer will probably depress you. But don't despair. There are several ways to **maximise the effectiveness** of your budget:

- You won't want to mail to everyone at the same time. There's probably little point in blowing all your ammunition in one shot, so do another little sum. Estimate how much you'll need to spend on each mailing (don't forget postage costs) and derive a figure for the number of people you can afford to mail at each 'drop'.

- It's all very well setting yourself a budget, but when will your cash flow best be able to bear the expenditure? Perhaps certain periods of the year, or even months, see most money coming in, and enable you to plan accordingly.

- Talk to Royal Mail. Find out what discounts they might be able to offer you and when.

- Do you have any good friends in the print trade who might be able to offer you a deal? Even if you don't, it's often worth talking to printers to find out when they would be most happy to receive your work. Perhaps they can foresee a slack period on the horizon and would be willing to negotiate a favourable price for your co-operation with their own work flow requirements.

You get the idea. A little thought can often minimise your expenditure and enable you to mail more prospects at one time, or alternatively, spend more on each one. Don't be afraid to wheel and deal and use some of your own ingenuity. Experience in the mailing business will progressively teach you more about economic modes of operation.

DECIDING BETWEEN CONTINUOUS OR OCCASIONAL CAMPAIGNS

Now you should be in a position to answer the question that was posed earlier. Do you run a steady, continuous mailing campaign on a weekly or monthly basis, for example? Is a series of 'commando raids' a better option? Are you going to go the seasonal route, taking advantage of known variations in your business at different times of the year?

Here are some of the factors you might wish to take into account. You may well think of others.

- Do you have a sales force or team of agents who need a steady flow of leads?

- Is there a seasonal factor in your busines? Christmas? Summer?

- What does your budget say? There's no point in mailing out a minuscule number of mailers each week when it would be more efficient to undertake two or three larger 'hits' at wider intervals.

- Are there foreseeable periods when your cash flow could do with a boost?

- Do you need leads NOW?

- Can your administrative structure handle a big inflow of leads arriving all at once?

Which brings us on to the next point.

GETTING YOUR INFRASTRUCTURE IN ORDER

It's absolutely vital that your office systems can cope with a mailing campaign from the outset. Your staff (if you have any) will need to be able to prepare your mailings ('stuffing' materials into envelopes, for example), make sure each mailer is addressed correctly and reaches the post on time for your chosen mailing date, and generally make an efficient job of your operation. Holidays might be a factor. These mundane things don't just happen by themselves: they need to be planned for. You may have to plan on taking on extra temporary help, which will, of course, affect your budget.

Similarly, you have to make sure that the replies you receive are processed efficiently. Nothing affects a potential sale worse than a tardy, uninformed or generally amateurish follow-up to a lead given to you in good faith.

For all you know, your prospect's need might be urgent. Or it might be an 'impulse' return which could well be forgotten three days after it's sent to you. Make sure you can handle the replies you get. Otherwise, there's no point bothering to mail in the first place.

Checking your computer system

You should also take a look at your computer system, even if it only consists of one modest PC. Most reasonable word processing systems will give you the basics these days: Mail Merge, for example, helps you address each individual letter from a pre-installed mailing list.

Again, software which enables you to maintain a database of names and addresses, taking account of alphabetical order and geography, is readily available. You'll also need a spreadsheet system so that you can, for example, measure the effectiveness of your mailing efficiently.

There's little point in going into great detail about this here, because things move so fast in the computer world that anything said here will be out of date and superseded before you read this. Have a word with your computer software supplier and see what's on offer.

CHECKLIST

- Decide your market (individuals or companies?)
  Use the checklist above for a better definition.

- Locate your market
  Trading estates? Housing estates?

- Define the geography
  Pore over the maps!

- Use your budget effectively
  Temper your enthusiasm and take a hard look at your budget.

- Continuous or occasional?
  Regular schedule or 'commando raids'?

- Get your infrastructure in order
  Are you set up to handle your campaign?

CASE STUDIES

Phil's business is seasonal

Phil is well aware that there are certain times of the year when business is slacker than others. He therefore decides to run carefully tailored mailers appropriate to the season, and not try to run a continuous campaign.

In summer, he often finds himself working outdoors, while internal decoration, for example, can be performed satisfactorily during the cold winter months. He therefore proposes to organise two 'outdoor' mailings in the spring, one 'indoor' mailing in the autumn, and one just after Christmas.

Howard needs a continuous flow of leads

Howard needs to keep his small sales force busy. He therefore decides on a monthly series of mailings, highlighting various products at different times. However, he isn't always going to know which products to 'push' until the mailing is a month or two away, so he needs to make sure he is geared to quick decisions, and a type of mailer which can be produced simply and quickly.

The one exception to this is that he needs to mail his company's annual catalogue in April, so he has to allocate extra funds to a more than usually extensive mailing.

Lynn goes the geographical route

Lynn has a wide geographical area to cover. She also has to consider two different objectives in her mailings. Her first aim is to raise much-needed funds for her charity, but she also needs to recruit more helpers in each region of her area. In some places she has more volunteers than in others.

She decides to run a system of regular mailings of two different sorts. She will split her area into several smaller sub-sections, based on the number of volunteers she can call upon. Where she is weak in that respect, she will mail with an emphasis on recruitment, where she has plenty of helpers she will go all out for fundraising. By working systematically through her various sub-areas she hopes to achieve both her objectives.

4

Deciding Where to Mail

If you've taken due note of the previous chapters then you will know a fair amount about your prospective customers by now. However, all the information you have needs to be pulled together so that you can decide on the **creative aspects** of your mailings.

'SEXING' YOUR PROSPECTS

In mailing terms, there are more than two sexes:

- male

- female

- juvenile

- a mixture.

If your market is predominately **male** (motorcycles, male cosmetics, male-oriented magazines, for example) then your mailers will be designed and written in a less feminine style than if it is **female** (needlework, fashion, romantic fiction).

If your audience is like to be **juvenile** or **teenage** (toys, games, pop music), then your creative parameters will change accordingly. But there's a complication.

Often, buying decisions for the juvenile market are made by adults. You know the sort of conversation: 'Gosh Mum, that's great! Can I have it?', 'No you can't! It's rubbish! Anyway, we can't afford it!'

In any case, you'll find it difficult to find or create a mailing list purely for that market. So usually, you'll be mailing to parents. Even then, there's a sexist element. Dads are more likely to be able to select the best constructional toy, for example, while Mums will know more about cookery and needlework.

A high proportion of mailings is really aimed at couples or

families. Buying a fitted kitchen, for example, is likely to be a joint decision. So you may be mailing to a **mixture** of people. Sometimes, as in deciding on a holiday, the whole family is involved, whereas the kids couldn't care less about home insurance.

But all these considerations have to be taken with a grain of salt. An aggressive motorcycle campaign might be macho in tone, but that would risk alienating female bikers. You may have to wear that to influence the majority. It's as well to be aware, however, that this factor does exist, and to take due account of it where you can.

MAILING TO INDIVIDUAL OR BUSINESS?

The approach made to individual and corporate prospects must necessarily be different. As discussed earlier, *the very same individual* presents differing problems when he is sitting at home with his family and when he is operating in his professional capacity. In many respects he is two completely separate personalities.

Generally speaking, a commercial prospect needs to be approached in a businesslike, professional manner. There is little scope for humour, for example – although that is not the same as saying that there is no scope at all. However, before you approach a commercial prospect in a lighthearted manner, you'd better be sure what you're doing.

When mailing to individuals, however, you can relax a little. Sometimes you can go all out to entertain, and you are not so constricted by the need to write in hard, business terms.

Much of this, of course, depends on your product. You wouldn't try to sell a funeral plan, for example, with a mailer featuring cartoon-type drawings. On the other hand, a holiday offer needs to be promoted in an attractive, even seductive, way without too much emphasis on the severe business pitch.

Some products do blur the lines a little. A travel agency offering incentive holidays for a company sales force has to be businesslike, but also needs to portray the luxury hotels and sun-drenched beaches.

You know your own business best and should use that knowledge before being swayed too much by the marketing pundits. It's like everything else in this business. The only hard and fast rule is that there are no hard and fast rules.

LOOKING AT INCOME AND GEOGRAPHY

The two do often go hand in hand. People with similar levels of disposable income tend to live in similar properties, which in turn tend to cluster together in localities and estates. This can help you with your mailing. You can write a suitable letter for, let's say, a large two and three bedroom out-of-town modern estate, and vary your approach when dealing with a Victorian development of older, smaller houses.

One pitfall to watch for is concerned with precisely these older developments. You might see a pleasant neighbourhood consisting of spacious Edwardian villas, only to find that they have all been subdivided into flats, some of which will house single-parent families, and even DSS claimants. A little investigation 'on the ground', if that's practicable, will soon establish the truth of the matter. Watch out for the array of entry buttons outside the front doors.

DEFINING YOUR PROSPECT'S PERSONALITY

The word 'personality' in this context means those factors which decide how he, she or they are influenced by your sales pitch. It's obvious, really. If you're selling fitted kitchens, the sheer luxury and attractiveness of a product will appeal to a senior manager on a high salary more than it will to someone who has to watch the pennies and is more interested in the utility and value for money represented by your offer.

There are many such factors. They include:

- income
- age range
- family circumstances
- ethnic origin
- profession
- sheer bloody-mindedness.

The list isn't exclusive, but it will do to be going on with.

Income is obvious. People with more money tend to buy more expensive things.

Age range is more complex. Not only is a young mum with a growing family likely to be interested in the convenience and labour-saving features of your product, but she is also liable to be influenced by the more trendy factors. Will the design of your product appeal to her more than to an older age group?

If the same young lady is still footloose and fancy-free, she is likely to be a little easier to sell to, simply because she probably isn't required, or isn't inclined, to think so hard about a purchase. Those were the days!

Good solid middle-aged people tend to have good, solid middle-aged preferences and prejudices when it comes to buying via direct mail.

Perhaps the most interesting age range at the beginning of the twenty-first century is the most senior one. Many over-60s have healthy disposable income, these days. Many struggle by on the state pension. They may live next door to each other, and may have done so for years. This makes life difficult for the company which wishes to sell to them by direct mail, but the situation can be eased by a careful selection of the mailing list (this will be discussed in the next chapter).

One word of warning about the over-60s. Being elderly doesn't mean being stupid. No one gets his bus pass but loses his marbles at the same time. One great way to lose sales to pensioners is to patronise them.

Never, never, underestimate the senior citizens of society. They didn't get where they are without gaining a lot of experience, and can probably spot a specious approach a mile off. They've been there, done that and probably *invented* the T-shirt.

Family circumstances have an enormous effect on the buying decision, possibly overriding all other considerations. Even the economic aspect might be outweighed, because a householder who knows very well that the item in question can't really be afforded can be persuaded by pleas from a partner or children. No one wants their kids to suffer by comparison with their peers in the playground, for example.

The converse can also be true. If a family have decided to go off on an expensive summer holiday, for example, then everyone might know very well that they have to save up for it, and will be more ready to forego that new dress or CD player.

If you are mailing to families then it is probably prudent to regard the buying decision as a joint one and to design and write accordingly.

Ethnic origin is regarded as a hot potato, but there's no need to get paranoid about it. The thing to remember is that each ethnic grouping has its own divisions, and even disagreements. The bland word 'Asian' can, for instance, cover anyone whose family roots stem from everywhere from China to Pakistan, and that's a healthy fraction of the world's population. It can even include people from Kenya or Uganda.

Even within a national grouping there are different sets of customs and values, and you can't be expected to know all the nuances involved, yet it's easy to offend someone quite innocently.

If you are mailing specifically to one ethnic grouping – Caribbean clothes or cosmetics, for example – and you don't happen to belong to that ethnic group yourself, then the thing to do is ask someone who does. There are always organisations, societies, clubs or even quangos whose advice can be sought. That can help you avoid pitfalls, and might even earn you brownie points among that community for having the sensitivity to seek it.

It has to be faced that differing ethnic groups have differing mind sets, and that is still true, in many cases, even if it was your prospect's grandfather who was the original emigrant.

You may, of course, be mailing to someone simply because of their *professional* status, in which case you'll know a lot about them before you start and there's no problem. But it's as well to remember that even though an individual's attitudes to buying via direct mail changes significantly when he gets home and puts his feet up, he can't discard all his training and experience completely.

An engineer tends to think in straight lines. An artist's thought processes are more convoluted and less disciplined in that sense.

Of course, some recipients of your mailing will simply be **bloody-minded** about the whole thing. There are people, usually individuals rather than commercial prospects, who are just not going to buy anything that they're told about by direct mail.

Forget 'em. They're fewer than you might think, and you have better fish to fry anyway.

CHOOSING THE STYLE: 'PLUSH', 'CHEAP AND CHEERFUL' OR 'BUSINESSLIKE'

The list of factors affecting your prospect's personality is longer than the one detailed above, of course. Political leanings, religious affiliations, heritage and upbringing all play a part, but the point is that you should have a long and hard think about the sort of person you are trying to influence. Having done that, and taken due account of the other topics discussed in this chapter, you can now decide on the **style of mailing** you might want to undertake.

And you have to do it at this point because the conclusions you come to affect averything else from here on. Your budget will be affected, and therefore the number of mailings you can afford. So let's take a look at your options.

Obviously, the nature of your product is a factor. No one is likely to pursue the purchase of an item costing thousands of pounds if he or she is introduced to it by a simple black-and-white, A5 flyer. The converse is also true. In some cases a plush mailing can provoke the reaction 'if they can afford all this posh literature, then they can't be all that hard up'.

Here's a very brief summation to get you thinking.

A **plush** mailing, one using heavy paper, full colour and loads of photographs, for example is appropriate where the product or service concerned is an expensive or luxurious one. If you are *offering* luxury, then your mailer should *reflect* that. There is also a snob factor. If you are offering prestige or appealing to vanity, then you should make that obvious from the word go.

Sometimes a degree of 'plushness' can't be avoided. Anyone selling plants for the garden or fashion accessories can't evade illustrating them in as flattering a light as possible.

Cheap and cheerful encompasses the vast area of products which are affordable, workaday or perhaps, like home insurance, say, unavoidable. Please note that, in this context, 'cheap' means inexpensive, not tawdry, and 'cheerful' means pleasant, not flippant.

This sort of mailing probably uses two or three colours, incorporates few illustrations and is printed on a good middle-of-the-road paper.

A **businesslike** mailer is the one which you send to business customers. It possibly consists of a well-written letter, a reply card and a piece of your standard literature which you use for general purposes.

However, this type of mailing is also widely used for a variety of household purposes, often those of a more 'serious' nature. Examples would include financial services, home maintenance and therapeutic products.

If in doubt, you can't go wrong by trying this approach.

CHECKLIST

- **Sexes:** is your market primarily among men, women, juniors, a mixture, and who is most likely to make the buying decision?

- **Commercial or consumer?** Are you in a 'business' or 'individual' market? Or are there elements of both?

- **Income and geography:** estimate the likely income range of your customers. Are there geographical areas where these prospects may be concentrated?

- **Personality:** take a hard look at the 'personality' of the prospects most likely to buy your product or service. In what 'tone of voice' should you be speaking to them?

- **'Plush', 'Cheap and cheerful', 'businesslike':** what sort of image should your mailing project? Luxurious, value for money or straightforward and businesslike?

CASE STUDIES

Phil decides to go the 'businesslike' route

Phil knows that most of his customers are likely to be from family homes, although he does get a fair amount of business from local firms. He is also aware that his services might involve a comparatively major investment for many people. He therefore decides to project a thoroughly trustworthy and no-nonsense image by using a carefully constructed letter with a reply-paid card for response.

Howard thinks he should project quality

Howard provides good quality products which do not have a particular price advantage over his competitors. His company has a reputation for reliability and helpfulness. He therefore decides that a colour, illustrated leaflet, bearing an appropriate letter, and accompanied by a reply card offering a range of sales literature should be his preferred option.

Lynn needs to be pleasant and efficient

Lynn needs to appeal to her audience's charitable instincts, but must beware of appearing too mawkish, or of implying that a large proportion of the donations received disappear into administration – such as the production of mailing material. She also knows that her best prospects are from among people with a healthy disposable income.

She therefore decides to produce a middle-of-the-road leaflet bearing an appeal letter with some colour and a modicum of illustration. She cannot use a reply card, because she wants people to send her donations. She therefore has to include a reply-paid envelope. As a result, she needs to include a name and address coupon on her mailer, rather than using a pre-addressed reply card.

5

Building a Mailing List

USING THE ROYAL MAIL

As a matter of fact, you may not need to 'build' a mailing list at all. The Royal Mail has perfectly efficient schemes to deliver your mailing for you, using the old, familiar postman. By that means you can cover **every address** in a specified geographical area with no bother at all.

Simple, isn't it? Give your local Royal Mail headquarters a ring and you'll find you get all the help and advice you need, delivered to you in a friendly and flexible manner.

Unfortunately, there's a major snag. All your mailers are delivered by address only, with no names involved. Your mailing is **not personalised** at all.

That may not worry you. Take-away food outlets, for example, are quite happy to blanket their immediate area simply to remind their potential customers that they are there, and to ensure that their telephone numbers are immediately to hand should anyone want to use their delivery service.

Many companies, however, do need to be sure that their offerings are addressed by name. Mailers labelled 'The Occupier', or something similar, have a much better chance of being thrown away unopened than ones that are personally addressed. The sheer immediacy of a letter with the recipient's name on it attracts much more attention than the impersonal nature of a communication which is obviously simply part of a blanket campaign.

Whether they know it or not, everyone takes more notice of a letter addressed to them personally.

In the commercial market there is simply no choice. If you can derive a list of business companies with your target executives addressed by name then that is by far the preferred option. Failing that, then mailers addressed to recipients by their job title is second best. So how do you set about building a mailing list?

USING EXISTING CUSTOMERS

It's one of the oldest sayings in marketing: 'Your best prospects are your existing customers.' Just because someone has done business with you before doesn't mean you should take him for granted.

In any case, your customers, even regular ones, may not be aware of the full range of your products or services. Even if that doesn't apply, you may be sure that your competitors will be out to poach your customers if they can, so it's only common sense to keep in touch with them.

The obvious place to start building your list is the list of customers you already have.

USING YOUR CONTACTS

Now, extend that thinking a little. You will have been in touch with a great many people with whom you have not, as yet, done business. You probably know people who have had contacts with you for other reasons – suppliers, service people, and the like. There will also be people who have sold, or tried to sell, something to *you*.

They're all grist to your mill. Go through your correspondence files, and include all the names therein on your mailing list. Don't try to make any judgements. Just put the lot in – and then set up an office system which ensures that anyone new with whom you are in contact, for any reason whatever, goes on your mailing list.

You can extend the thinking even further. You don't actually spend 24 hours a day at your job. You will have social contacts, you may be a member of various organisations, and you're always likely to be meeting new people. Put them all on your list.

If you are a member of some organisation, have a word with the secretary. You may well be able to acquire a copy of the membership list, perhaps in return for a donation to club funds. There's nothing unethical about this: it goes on all the time. Some organisations make very useful money by making their lists available for direct mail.

USING DIRECTORIES AND HANDBOOKS

Obviously, publications such as the telephone directory and *Yellow Pages* are fruitful sources of appropriate names and addresses. It can be a tedious job to extract the ones you want, but worth the effort. You should be aware, however, that the very nature of this type of publication means that it has a long lifetime, and, just as important, a long lead-time in its preparation. This means that the names and addresses you extract may not be right up to date. People do move on.

You'll find that your local reference library has a wide selection of trade and professional directories with all the names and addresses you could ever want categorised. You may not want to spend many hours in the library poring over such publications, but you can find out what is available, and then purchase the directories which apply to your particular business.

Don't forget that most professions have their own handbook listing those qualified to be members. The clergy, for example, are listed in *Crockfords*. Again, such handbooks are valuable.

Using electorial rolls

If your requirement is geographical, that is if you want to mail to all individuals in a given area, take a look at the **electoral rolls**. These are usually produced according to local government ward boundaries, and typically contain around 3–4,000 names.

Your local council will sell you copies of the ones you want, and some authorities are now supplying them on CD, which is useful.

One little point. Electoral rolls indicate young people who reach the age of 18, and therefore qualify to vote, during the year of currency of the roll by putting their birthdate against their names. That could come in handy if you have an appropriate product.

Electoral rolls are compiled from returns to a mailing sent out to everyone in the district in October. They are usually produced early in the following year – so perhaps that is the best time to purchase them.

Of course, not everyone makes sure that his or her name is on the electoral roll, even though it is technically an offence to fail to send in a return. That figure is inclined to drop when everyone knows that a general election may be imminent.

Nevertheless, the electoral roll is a very useful, and very available, source of information.

USING OTHER SOURCES

Once you become sensitive to the need to acquire lists of names you'll be surprised just how many sources there are. It's a question of being alert to opportunities. Here are a few possibles, and once you have the idea, you'll come across others.

- local trades directories

- advertisements in your local papers and free sheets

- direct mail you receive yourself

- public service announcements in the local press

- fascias over shops in high streets and shopping centres

- firms occupying office blocks (look at the list in the vestibule).

One very popular method of building a mailing list involves participating in local shows, fairs and exhibitions. A typical operation consists of taking space at, say, a trades show. You then attract visitors to the stand with a display of products, which ensures that all your patrons are, at least, interested in what you have to offer. Once there, your visitors are inveigled into taking part in a free daily lottery (bottles of wines and spirits are popular for this). To do this, they have to complete a card with their names and address details, so that the winner's prize can be passed on later. *Et voila! A mailing list!*

A variation is to make your lottery a paid affair, from which all the proceeds go to a suitable charity. You get your list, the charity gets a donation, and everyone is happy.

On general principles, if you are taking part in any show, then the names and addresses of all visitors should be taken if at all possible.

BUYING A LIST

You can use all the methods above to build a list, but in the earlier stages at least we are talking about relatively small numbers, probably in the low thousands. Furthermore, it may be a fairly slow process. These factors may not worry you, depending on your geographical limitations and the number of leads you need or can service efficiently.

If you require larger numbers of prospects, or perhaps more highly qualified ones – freelance accountants working from home, for example – then it is perfectly possible to buy virtually any list you can think of. Many companies exist which will be only too happy to fulfil your requirements, and many of those will handle the whole direct mail operation for you if you prefer.

There are some very good, highly professional, direct mail companies about who offer the complete service from initial concept through writing, design and printing to mailing and processing of leads received. They have to be good, or they wouldn't survive in a very competitive market indeed.

Finding lists for sale

Let's assume, for the moment, that all you need is to purchase a mailing list.

Your first stop could well be your *Yellow Pages* or similar publication. You will almost certainly find companies listed who will be happy to supply the list you need.

Even better would be a brief search on the Internet, about which more later. The World Wide Web will show you far more such companies than you ever need, some generalist, some specialised. Simply use a search engine, such as 'Ask Jeeves' and you'll be given details of more list suppliers than you can shake a reply card at.

The snag, of course, is that buying a list can be expensive. At least, it looks that way, but if you take into account the equally expensive time spent by you and your staff in creating and collating your own list, then perhaps it needn't be as uneconomic as it looks at first sight.

Another advantage to buying a list is that it will have been professionally compiled and maintained: that is, it will have been regularly 'cleaned' to remove redundant and duplicated entries.

Lists can be purchased in any form suitable for your own particular requirements: on labels, floppy disks or CD. Remember: labels once used are gone. Lists on floppies or CD are a thing of beauty and a joy forever.

The company would probably want to see specimens of your proposed mailings, just to make sure that you're not issuing anything illegal, offensive or libellous. But that's not unreasonable, is it?

USING COMPUTERS

It's a little difficult to give hard-and-fast advice on computerised direct mail systems simply because the whole field changes and develops so quickly. Today's wonder of the world is *passé* tomorrow. By the time you read this it will probably be possible to acquire a software system which can handle the whole operation of a direct mail campaign from beginning to end.

Certain things can still be said, however. If all you have is a fairly minimal PC system, required only as a word processor and, perhaps, to look after your accounting, then you probably already have the basic tools to record and maintain a mailing list. Basically, you need:

- a word processor
- a database system
- a spreadsheet system
- a good quality printer.

You can certainly get by just with those minimal facilities. If you are thinking of handling relatively small numbers of mailings at any one time, then you might like to consider adding:

- a higher quality colour printer, designed to provide reasonably large numbers of copies
- a scanner, so that you can reproduce your own illustrations
- Desk Top Publishing software.

Please do remember, however, to keep back-up copies of all your material, including your list, on floppy disks. If you lost your hard drive through some virus or other mishap you'd be tearing your hair out for weeks.

MAKING THE MOST OF THE INTERNET

The Internet is an enormously powerful tool with tremendous potential in all sorts of fields, and that includes direct mail. You could certainly, with a little experience and ingenuity, use it to derive a mailing list: indeed so much information is available through the World Wide Web that your major problem could well be sorting the wheat from the chaff.

Many well-informed authorities consider that every business will have Internet access in the near future, simply because it will be impossible to do business without it. Thereafter, virtually every household will be 'on the net', in the same way that almost everyone has a telephone.

Various attempts are being made to control the Internet, but they are probably doomed to fail. To a large extent the would-be controllers are up against the laws of physics, and no one ever won that battle yet.

If you are not yet wired into the Internet, then you are strongly advised to remedy that omission as soon as you can. You'll find it a tool useful in your mailing activities and in many other spheres. The ability to e-mail prospects, customers and others is a huge asset to any company, and gets more important all the time.

Don't be afraid of it. Once you have Internet access you'll be operating like a veteran within minutes, or certainly an hour or two. It really isn't difficult, even if you are a complete computer ignoramus.

And don't be afraid of the cost. It is extremely easy to acquire free Internet access from an ever-growing number of sources. You needn't be nervous about your phone bill either. All Internet connections are made at local phone call rate, and even that is eroding. At least one Internet Service Provider is negotiating to use an '0800' phone number at the time of writing, so it may be all completely free before very long.

If your office computer doesn't have a modem, then get one installed. And then start ringing round to find free Internet access.

MAINTAINING YOUR LIST

Lists, like other things, are quite capable of going past their sell-by dates. People move house, change jobs, move within their companies, and generally make life difficult for anyone trying to maintain an up-to-date mailing list. It is therefore important to make efforts to 'clean' your list as well as you can.

Every time you get a response from your mailing, check the original list entry to see if the information you now have is the same as originally entered. If you are using the electoral roll, buy another one next year.

You probably won't be able to maintain your list as well as a professional direct mail organisation does, but at least you must be conscious of the problem, and do what you can to alleviate it.

6

Producing a Basic Mailer

First, last and always, direct mail is a *personal* medium. Anything which comes through your letterbox at home, with your name on it, 'hits you where you live' quite literally.

In a different sort of sense, this is equally true of mailers sent to commercial organisations. Anything which arrives on an executive's desk, even if addressed to the recipient only by job title, is an uninvited invasion of personal space.

It is this factor which gives direct mail its unique impact – its ability to **demand** attention where other media only attract passing interest. It is also the source of most of the pitfalls in the direct mail process, because a reader can dismiss the contents of an advertisement, for instance, as not really being intended for him or her, but there's no escape from a personally addressed letter.

So you'd better get your mailing right. The effect of a mistake in an advertisement is probably merely neutral, whereas a poor mailer can actually prejudice the prospective customer against the product being promoted.

WRITING THE BASIC DIRECT MAIL LETTER

The word to remember is *personal*. Every mailing should be personalised as far as possible preferably by using the prospect's name, possibly a job description, perhaps by using a 'Dear Sir/ Madam', or if all else fails, 'To the Occupier'. Anything which does not carry this personalisation isn't a mailer at all. It's just a leaflet.

If you think about it, this implies that an actual letter is an essential element of any direct mail package. Please note, however, that the letter does not have to stand entirely on its own. It could, for example, be the front page of a four-page brochure.

Making your letter stand out

So how do you set about writing a good direct mail letter? Let's start from the top. With your letterhead.

You'll probably be more familiar with your **letterhead** than with any other element of your office stationery. You may have been using it for years. It's familiar and comfortable. Why change it?

There may be no reason for change at all, but there are one or two elements which are worth inspecting from a mailing point of view. For one thing, the last thing you want on a direct mail letterhead is clutter. While a nice piece of design running down one edge of the paper may be fine for general correspondence use, it will simply get in the way of your mailer's message, distracting attention just when that's the last thing you want to happen.

This doesn't mean that you have to throw your existing letterheads away: you can go on using them just as you have always done. It could just be, however, that it would be a good idea to design a special letterhead for use with direct mail.

Case study

Don't be misled into thinking that it isn't worth going to that sort of effort 'just for a few mailers'. One very large multinational company with British headquarters in Middlesex learned that lesson some years ago.

They spent a considerable amount of money updating all their stationery, using the services of a sophisticated company specialising in such services. Everyone liked the results, until early samples arrived on the desk of the copywriter responsible for producing the organisation's direct mail letters. He felt that the whole system was too rigid and didn't offer him the flexibility he felt he needed.

The company's management shrugged him off with the statement that to accede to his request for amendments would be 'making the tail wag the dog'.

Feeling slightly aggrieved, he then pointed out that he was responsible for some *four million* letters being posted each year, and that that was more than all the other correspondence sent out by the company put together.

Back, as they say, to the old drawing board.

So here are some elements of a good direct mail letterhead.

- Use **A4 paper**, and print your details straight across the top. Get them into one, two, or at the most, three lines. Choose an interesting but **unfussy** typeface.

- Draw a **rule**, right across the page below the address details to prevent distracting the eye too much away from your story.

    The end result might look something like this:

STRAWBURY OFFICE SUPPLIES,
12 New Street, Strawbury, Beds. B15 X2Q
Tel: 01999 123 456. Fax: 01999 123 457

- **Take a look at colours, too**. Don't use more than two colours in your letterhead, possibly only one.

    One good tip, particularly if you are on a tight budget, is – don't use black as your letterhead colour. If you use any other colour, and produce your letter in the conventional black, then you automatically get a two-colour job. You can then use a third colour for the signature.

    Don't forget that there's no law which says your notepaper must be white. An enormous range of colours is available these days, often no more expensive than the familiar white.

- And talking of **paper**, it may be that you can use a lighter, and hence less expensive, paper for your mailers than you do for your general correspondence.

STARTING YOUR LETTER

Address
No mystery about where to start. You start with the **recipient's address**.

If you know the name of your prospect, then you start your address lines with it in just the way you would in any normal business correspondence. If you don't, then use the job description of the official you are trying to reach, if you're in the commercial market.

If you're simply 'blanketing' an area, perhaps with the aid of the Royal Mail, then you may not be using names, addresses and descriptions at all. In that case you are forced into the bland 'The

Occupier' or 'The Householder' but please do insert *something*. If you are tempted to go straight into the body of your letter, then you are losing some of the personalisation which is the great strength of the direct mail medium.

Date

For the same reason, you should always insert a date. However, it's just as well to give yourself a little leeway for a variety of reasons. You may not be sending out all your offerings on the same day. You won't want to undertake a whole series of printings just because the dates vary, for example.

The convention is simply to indicate the month of the mailing, *eg* 'July 2000', and there isn't really any reason to depart from that.

Salutation

'Dear . . .'

Your salutation needs thinking about. If you know your prospect's name and he happens to be male, then there's no problem: 'Dear Mr Bunberry' (or whatever) does the job perfectly. The female of the species is a little more difficult because you probably won't know whether she likes to be addressed as 'Mrs', 'Miss', or 'Ms'. The solution is to use 'M/s' which covers the whole thing.

Very frequently, of recent years you'll see the use of a simple first name and surname, for example, 'Belinda Bunberry'. Many ladies seem to like this mode of address, so you can use it if you know it. Quite a lot depends on the formality of your approach. If you think 'stiff and starch' is your preferred tone of voice, then use the honorific. If you're trying to be friendly, then go the first and surname route.

If you are writing to a business address, then if you know the executive's name, there isn't any problem. If you don't then you can probably use the job description – 'Dear Catering Manager', for instance.

To be strictly accurate, a simple 'Dear Sir' should be suitable for everyone under correct English usage, because the masculine embraces the feminine, as we used to be taught at school.

Nowadays, however, in our politically correct society, the whole matter needs a little thought.

WRITING AN EFFECTIVE DIRECT MAIL LETTER

Here's where you should be introduced to AIDA. Most people call her 'Ada', although there are those who prefer the operatic pronunciation.

AIDA is a venerable old lady, now, having come to the aid of generations of direct mail writers. In fact, she has been around for so long precisely because she is so good at what she does. And that is helping you to write effective letters.

AIDA stand for four words:

- Attract

- Interest

- Desire

- Action.

Let's explain.

Attract

You have very little time in which to attract the attention of your reader. His attention must be held right from the moment he starts to read. If not, then he won't bother to finish the letter, and it will go straight into the bin. So you need what is known as a 'fish hook', that is a device to capture the prospect's attention from the word 'go'.

The very best word with which to 'hook' your reader is the word 'You'. Examples of how to use it would be 'You will be interested to learn that . . .' or 'You have the chance to save money on a whole range of . . .'.

It isn't necessary to go overboard about this. Sometimes it may be preferable to use some such device as 'As a leading company in your field, you will be interested in . . .'

Never, ever start your letter with the words 'I' or 'We'. A lengthy screed full of 'we did this' and 'we did that' is one of the surest turn-offs in the business. So much so that there is a name for such missives in the business. They're called 'Wee Wee Letters'.

Put yourself in the prospect's shoes

The reason for all this is encapsulated in another useful acronym:
UTGP

This does not, as has been unkindly suggested, stand for 'Up the Garden Path', but '**Understand the Guy's Problem**'.

Of course, the guy might be a girl, but the principle is sound. UTGP tells you to put yourself in your prospect's shoes, and focus on what he or she really wants or needs.

Your reader isn't in the least interested in your problems. He has enough of his own.

However, there are times when you may wish to use 'I' or 'We'. Towards the end of your letter, once you've made your sales pitch, you may wish to assure your future customer of your best attention at all times, or that you will personally ensure that his valued enquiry will be dealt with immediately. In that case the first person pronoun is entirely appropriate.

But please do start your letter with that word **YOU**.

It's the one most likely to grab your prospect's attention.

Interest

So now you have your reader's attention. The next trick is to hold it, and to interest him in the product or service you are selling.

Here's where you spell out your story, giving as much detail as you think proper of your proposition. Again, remember UTGP. Put yourself in his position, and try to understand what he wants from you. You may not, in fact, be selling what you think you are.

For example:

- You don't sell burglar alarms, you sell **security**.

- You don't sell decoration or decoration materials, you sell an **attractive home**.

- You don't sell stationery supplies, you sell a better **company image** and absolute **reliability of supply**.

Some companies, however, do have to be careful of what some people call a 'distress sale', that is something everyone has to have but doesn't really want. We all, for example, have to have house insurance, but we'd rather not. Most of the time it seems like money poured into a black hole, so we'd rather not think about it.

In that case, the insurers would probably focus on a price advantage or prompt settlement of claims, or something similar.

There is always a way round these things. You just have to think about it.

Understand the guy's problem!

Desire

Here's where you start to move in for the kill. Here's where you take the interest you have created and convert it into 'I've gotta have that!' or perhaps 'I'd better know more about that'.

You have several ways of doing that. You may have kept one of your best selling points back for just this moment. You may reiterate something you have already said with greater emphasis, or displayed in an eye-catching way. You may be making your prospect a special offer – one that you hope he can't refuse.

We'll go into this in more detail a little later, but now's the time to start thinking about your clincher.

Action

So now you've attracted your reader's attention, you've created interest in what you have to offer, and you've reinforced this to the extent that your prospect really wants to know more about your product or service. Now you have to tell him **what to do**.

This is important. It's an old salesman's cliché that more sales are lost by not asking for the order than for any other reason. Transferring this thinking to the direct mail context, it is fatally easy to get the prospect on your side and then lose him by not giving precise, simple directions about where he goes from here.

So what *do* you want him to do?

- Return the enclosed reply-paid card?
- Ring me on . . . ?
- E-mail me at . . . ?
- Fill in the coupon and return in the reply-paid envelope provided?
- Place your business card in the enclosed envelope and pop it in the post?
- Or a choice of some or all of these?

Whatever you decide, some such direction simply has to be given at this point if you wish to maximise the response to your mailing.

Asking more than once

Some pundits maintain that you should 'ask for the order' in this way three times in any direct mail letter. At the beginning, middle and end. You may well find, however, that this is once too many because the continual repetition of the direction to action gets in the way of the primary message you are trying to impart.

If you think you can get away with it expeditiously, then by all means try it, but don't think the triple direction to action is a hard and fast rule. It isn't.

You can, however, get your direction in twice – once at the beginning and once at the end of your letter. Having written your initial attention getter, you could, for example, continue by saying something like:

'The enclosed reply-paid card gives you a simple and convenient way of receiving more information.'

You would then conclude your letter by writing:

'Return the reply card today. You have nothing to lose and a very great deal to gain.'

You see the idea. You'll certainly be able to adapt it for your own use.

INSERTING ATTENTION GETTERS

Have you noticed that many direct mail letters use a line space rather than an indentation to indicate paragraphs? In other words a paragraph looks like this

rather than looking like this. One reason for the choice is because the company concerned likes to reserve indentation for emphasis rather than as a method of punctuation.

If your letter occupies most of an A4 page, and it probably will, a solid mass of unrelieved copy can be a little off-putting. An 'attention getter' can relieve the eye, attract interest and also give you a chance to emphasise what you believe to be your strongest selling point. Placing indentations breaks up the straight line of type on the left-hand side of the page and makes the letter just that much easier to read. Remember, the indented paragraph will have a line space above and below it.

Now take that thinking a little further. You can increase emphasis by indenting *and* using bold type.

You could also use italics, giving even more emphasis to your indentation and bold type.

YOU COULD EVEN USE UPPER CASE, THAT IS, CAPITAL LETTERS.

AND, OF COURSE, THERE IS ALWAYS UNDERLINING.

Printing your attention-getting paragraph in a second colour is another option. It is probably going a bit far to try to use all these options at the same time, but by combining them you have a great deal of flexibility in the way you emphasise your strongest point. The case histories at the end of this chapter will give you some concrete examples.

USING THE P.S.

Oddly enough, although we tend to regard the traditional 'P.S.' at the end of a letter as simply an afterthought, it makes a very good attention getter in its own right. It can be used to reiterate, and therefore emphasise, something you've said already – 'Do ring me today – I shall look forward to hearing from you', for example. It also gives you a handy method of introducing a topic that wouldn't fit easily into the main body of your letter, something like – 'Why not drop in and see us at our stand at the local Trades Council Exhibition, The Leisure Centre, 23 May' perhaps.

You can use any of the options illustrated above for your P.S., but there is another intriguing possibility. Why not reproduce your short message in a facsimile of your own handwriting, followed by your initials?

Now that really does look as if you are taking a personal interest in your reader.

INCLUDING THE ESSENTIAL REPLY ELEMENT

It was stated earlier that the only rule about direct mail is that there are no hard and fast fules. This is true, and that statement includes the rule that there are no hard and fast rules. The exception that proves it is as follows, and it is so important that it is worth stating with as much emphasis as possible.

• **Never, NEVER, NEVER issue a mailer without including a reply element**.

Always make it as easy as possible for your recipient to reply. The best method is to use a **reply-paid card**, but in some cases you may need to employ a **reply-paid envelope**, possibly because you are asking for a cheque to be sent to you, or because the reply involves sending you some information that your correspondent wouldn't want displayed openly for all to see, such as income details.

Sometimes, you may think it sufficient to ask your reader to ring or e-mail you. This is not ideal, but if you have constraints on your budget or the time scale involved you might be forced into it.

If you do decide to go this route, then don't be tempted to ask the reader to 'ring me at the number above' relying on your letterhead to do the job for you. It's much better to quote the number or e-mail address again at the appropriate point in the letter. This is because readers who have to flick their eyes from the bottom to the top of the page have had their attention distracted. And that's the last thing you want.

Some people, handling relatively small numbers of mailers, use the device of saying something like 'Please ring me on ABCDE FGHIJK. If I don't hear from you by the end of the month, I'll give myself the pleasure of ringing you.'

That can be very effective, because it gives you the chance to talk to your prospect, and anything is better than a cold call as any salesman will tell you.

Even if your prospect can't remember receiving your letter, you still have an 'in', because you can then say something like: 'Oh! Thank goodness I rang you. I wouldn't want you to miss out on something as good as this!'

Just one thing. If you do promise to ring your prospect, then you'd better be sure you do. For all you know, he may have taken note of your offer to call him and is sitting back waiting for you to do so. If you don't . . . Well, it doesn't bear thinking about.

Using reply-paid cards

Far from being simply a method of reply, a reply-paid card can augment the selling process by involving the prospect personally in your offer.

Some years ago a large West Midlands company sent out a round mailer. One of the reasons their advertising agency suggested it was to enable the enclosed reply-paid card to read 'Thank you for your circular'.

It worked very well. The prospect felt he was in on the joke when he returned the card.

You might not want to go quite that far, but you can usually involve your prospect in some way or another. Something like: 'Yes! I have a problem. Please send me your literature.'

(On that point, you don't necessarily have to put the required literature in the post. It might be better to send it clutched in the hot little hand of a representative.)

Your reply card is also a great source of information. By asking the right questions you can find out just what his requirement is. Which of several product lines does he want, for example?

This information can be used to refine your mailing list and target your mailers more accurately in future campaigns. It can also be used to 'clean' your list. Perhaps there is a new occupant of the property you were mailing to, for instance.

Returned cards will also give you a way to acquire names where you only had a job description. That can't be bad.

Improving the level of response
Just one more thing. By addressing your reply card, instead of, or as well as, your letter, you have made life much easier for your prospect. He doesn't even have to add a name and address, and can simply post the card with no effort whatsoever. It has been amply proved, over the years, that this does improve the level of response.

However, if you do address your card, please remember to include space elsewhere for 'Please enter your name and address details if different from shown on the left'.

As has been said before, things and personalities do change.

Using reply-paid envelopes

If you have to use a reply-paid envelope rather than a card, then you will have had to provide a coupon, or some other device, for your recipient to enter his or her details. However, you will have to have your reply envelope printed, so you can always maximise its usefulness by adding another message. The simple shout of URGENT! on an envelope can imply that you are going to give immediate attention to its contents.

And you are, aren't you?

CHECKLIST

- Is your letterhead flexible enough?
- How are you going to address your reader?
- UTGP (do you really know what your prospect wants?)
- Do you understand **AIDA?**
- Have you an 'attention getter'?
- Have you considered your reply element?
- Are you making the most of reply cards and envelopes?

CASE STUDIES

Phil wants to put a message on his letterhead

QRE BUILDERS

17 Brick Lane, Bilbury, Bucks. BY1 0ZZ Tel: 00000 00000

——————— Quality ◆ Reliability ◆ Economy ———————

Mr. T. Houseman
39 Mayflower Avenue,
Bilbury, Bucks

Howard decides to be straightforward and businesslike

BLACKBURY OFFICE SUPPLIES

23 Blackbury Square, Blackbury BX0 ZQ2. Tel 00000 000000

The Office Manager,
Toggle Flange Ltd.
Flange Works,
Brick Lane
Bluebury BZ2 3QP

Lynn needs to reflect the nature of her charity

FUW

Fund for URBAN wildlife

101, Fritillary Lane, Loganberry, Cambs. LB0 0ZZ
Tel 00000 00000

Mr. T. Gardener,
31, Thrush Meadow,
Bluberry,
Beds
5BB 0QQ

7

Making an Offer

So now you know just about everything about the mailer you are going to issue. But are you sure you will make your prospects really *want* to send back their reply?

If you are certain that the products or services you are offering can stand on their own, representing unusual value for money, unique quality or some other unmissable benefit, then all well and good. However, being painfully honest, are you really certain you can claim those things?

If not, then you need what is known in some circles as a 'widget'.

UNDERSTAND WIDGETS

A widget is something which adds that little extra to a mailing. Something which is offered to the reader as an extra reason to reply, quite apart from the main offer. It could be:

- a free gift
- a self-liquidator
- a useful or attractive piece of literature
- an offer of service
- or anthing else you can think of, really.

Free gifts

It is popularly held that the most effective word in the whole lexicon of advertising and promotion is that word FREE. Whatever the truth of that, the offer of something for nothing certainly appeals to everyone.

In this context your free gift in exchange for replying to your mailing could be anything relevant to your field, but of course, you do have to be able to afford it. The most inexpensive thing you have to give away is your own product.

Let's explain that. If you are selling, let's say, calendars, that cost you £1.00 each from your supplier, you may be selling them for around £2.50. Therefore, if you are giving away a £1 calendar, then the *perceived value* to the recipient is £2.50.

Now isn't that generous of you!

But don't forget to include postage and packing of your free gift in your costings.

Self-liquidators

You know the sort of thing. You see self-liquidators on such products as packs of tea or cereal boxes all the time. If someone offers to sell you a teacup and saucer for a ridiculously low price and a pack top or two, then that's a self-liquidator.

It's quite simple, really. The manufacturer buys a large quantity of some attractive item, getting the best price he can, and offers them to his customers at that unit price plus a little for overheads.

Self-liquidators can, of course, come from your own product range, which makes things simple. Alternatively, you will find promotional gift specialists in *Yellow Pages* (or on the Internet), and they are professionals at finding a constant supply of new and intriguing widgets. In addition, most large manufacturers in the consumer field have a promotional gift department or, at least, a system for supplying such items.

However, there are pitfalls in the self-liquidating field. You need to be sure of your source of supply, in case you get a larger response to your mailing than you anticipate. Conversely, you don't really want to be left with a pile of unclaimed items – although it may be perfectly possible to offer them again at a later date.

So you need to do your homework.

Literature

An offer of sales literature can be surprisingly effective, especially in the commercial field, where purchasers do like to keep up with what is currently on offer. In those cases, a '36-page, full-colour catalogue' has undeniable attraction, especially in connection with a persuasive mailing.

There are, of course, other forms of literature too. Calendars, diaries, year-to-view wall charts are just a few. You'll know what is appropriate in your own field, and it might be worth asking your suppliers what they can offer you. For free, of course.

Offer of service

Perhaps you are selling services rather than products. But that doesn't preclude you from using a widget. You could, perhaps, offer a free survey, a demonstration, a special price in return for the reply. There are plenty of alternatives and, once you start thinking about it, you'll find something appropriate for your own circumstances.

. . . or anything else, really.

All sorts of people are thinking of new types of widget all the time. There is probably no reason why you can't think of your own innovation.

CHECKLIST

- Do you need a 'widget'?
- If so, what form should it take?
  - free gift
  - self-liquidator
  - literature
  - service
  - your own bright idea.

CASE STUDIES

Phil decides to offer a free survey

In his trade, Phil is probably going to have to do a survey of the premises in which he is to work in any case, but the offer of doing one for free without any obligation on the part of his potential customer does seem attractive.

Phil also knows that there is a significant number of senior citizens in the area to which he is to mail. He therefore decides to offer special prices to OAPs.

Howard sees the chance to distribute his new catalogue

A mass distribution of Howard's new catalogue would be inherently wasteful because it would mean supplying an expensive piece of literature to a lot of people who aren't in the least interested in it. By offering it with his mailing he knows it will go to the right prospects, because it will only be sent to people who ask for it.

Lynn uses pictures to attract new members

Lynn's primary objective in her first mailing is to persuade people to join her charity. She has available a set of colour pictures of garden birds. These, she believes, would made an attractive incentive for people who need just that little extra stimulus to join up.

8

Anyone Can Be a Writer

Let's just pause there. It's all very well banging on about all the things you can do to run a successful direct mail operation, but what about the actual *writing*?

Surely all the advice and help in the world won't help if the writer has trouble stringing a few paragraphs together in a persuasive and attractive manner?

That's probably true, but virtually everyone can write acceptably if they really want to. It's rather like public speaking: some people have a natural aptitude for it, but anyone can do it if they put their mind to it. The problem is that most people are, quite needlessly, frightened of it. We can't all be Ernest Hemingways, but we can write quite well enough to make a success of it in this field, anyway.

KNOWING WHERE TO START

Terry Pratchett, arguably the funniest writer in English, has a word of advice for aspiring young writers who ask for the benefit of his wisdom.

'Let grammar and punctuation enter your life', he tells them.

Of course, he's right, but there's no need to get hidebound about it. In English we have the most flexible and useful language in the world with which to work. We don't pay it any compliment by lacing it into a straitjacket.

Sounds subversive, doesn't it? You can just see your old English teacher starting to go into a tizzy.

The thing to remember is that for practical purposes, there are two distinct and separate English languages: the written one and the spoken one. For our purposes, the latter is infinitely more useful. Copywriting has been called **indirect selling**, and that's not a bad definition. Direct selling is about meeting someone and talking them into buying a product. The closer you can get to that situation with your written material, the more likely you are to succeed.

Try this exercise. The next time you go down to the pub or club or wherever you do your socialising, sit quietly and just listen to people talk. You may find it a revelation. People don't converse grammatically. Sentences, and even paragraphs, are frequently started with 'Ands' and 'Buts', many so-called sentences aren't anything of the sort, but simply fragments, and a whole host of enormities are perpetrated on the language of the purists.

Not that there's anything wrong with being an English language purist. He is one of the highest forms of animal life. But (!) the point is this:

- You are not in the business of writing beautiful English. You are in the business of **selling things**, which means writing for meaning and impact.

How do I set about that?

One commonly used method is to find out as much as you can about the person to whom you are writing. If you've gone through the processes outlined in the first half of this book, then you have already done that, and you know a great deal about your prospect.

You then imagine that that person is sitting on the other side of your desk. Start writing in exactly the same way you would speak to him – or her.

Of course, it's not quite as simple as that. Let's get back to Mr Pratchett.

RECAPPING ON GRAMMAR AND PUNCTUATION

You do have to 'let grammar and punctuation enter your life'. In the spoken language those things are almost non-existent, but they do have to appear on the written page. Someone may well pause while they are speaking, but what does that pause represent in written terms? Comma? Semicolon? Colon? Dash? Full stop and new sentence? Paragraph?

The answer is that, as the writer, it's entirely up to you. The longer the pause you wish to indicate, the further up the scale you proceed. If your written pause signifies the introduction of a new topic or idea, then go for a new sentence or paragraph.

The comma does seem to be overused these days. The rule of thumb is, if in doubt, use a longer pause.

Paragraphs

As you may have noted earlier, in direct mail terms, the paragraph is more than just a punctuation device for changing the subject or indicating a long pause. It is also a way to make your letter more attractive to read. By splitting your letter into bite-sized chunks you make it much more digestible for your reader to work through than a solid mass of copy.

It's probably not wise to use more than six or seven lines in a single paragraph, and it's also a good idea to vary paragraph length if you can. That way your letter remains easy on the eye, and attracts the reader that much more efficiently.

The awful apostrophe

For some years there has been a trend to misuse the apostrophe. Yet there is nothing more calculated to make your letter look amateurish than a whole rash of the wretched things, popping up like acne. There does seem to be a school of thought which says 'if in doubt, bung in an apostrophe'.

This should be firmly avoided. The rules are simple: an apostrophe should only be used for two purposes, the possessive, and the abbreviation.

A *possessive* apostrophe indicates that something belongs to something or someone. Apostrophe-s ('s) is singular, as in 'the player's boot' while s-apostrophe (s') is plural, as in 'the players' boots'.

An apostrophe is also used to indicate *abbreviation*, as in 'Can't' for 'cannot' or 'shouldn't' for 'should not'.

These are the only times an apostrophe should be used. Anything else is simply wrong and looks terrible.

There is just one trap worth mentioning because even the best and most experienced copywriters fall into it occasionally. 'It's' means 'it is' and never 'belonging to it'. Do watch out for it. It's fatally easy to miss.

However, this is not supposed to be a treatise on English grammar and apologies are due to any grandmothers whose eggs we are describing how to suck. If you really are uneasy about it, then invest in a copy of *Fowler's Modern English Usage* which any large bookshop will be able to find for you. You might find it a daunting tome, but there is no better source for dipping into should you need to answer a grammatical question.

Spelling

You need to get it right. No one is a perfect speller, and all writers have the odd blind spot here and there. Your word processing system will probably provide you with a spellcheck program, and that will, of course, field most errors and correct typing mistakes too. However, it's not wise to rely on it completely.

A spellchecker won't usually pick up a misspelling which results in another perfectly valid word, typing 'blank' for example, when you meant to say 'black'.

Far better to go back to the bookshop again and acquire a decent dictionary. The *Concise Oxford Dictionary* is ideal, but there are several others.

LEARNING FROM OTHERS

So writing your own direct mail is nothing to worry about. Obviously, some people have a great flair for it and others don't, but you'll find you can make a perfectly acceptable job of it if you're not afraid to try. And don't be shy about stealing other writers' ideas. This is one field where people faced with similar problems come up with similar answers.

Why not start making a collection of mailers you receive yourself? You'll find a great deal of ammunition which you can use in your own campaigns.

Above all, don't get all hung up with matters of grammar and punctuation. You do have to know the rules before you can break them with impunity, but you learned them at school, anyway.

It's the overall impression that your mailer leaves in the recipient's mind which is important, and that isn't helped by a nit-picking insistence on getting every last rule of grammar absolutely right.

One of the finest copywriters that Britain ever produced used to have a saying about this. He used to tell young writers:

'If you take a watch to pieces you get an awful lot of interesting bits. But it won't tell time any more.'

CASE STUDIES

Phil, Howard and Lynn each produced mailing letters using different elements discussed in this chapter. See pages 77 to 79.

QRE BUILDERS

17 Brick Lane, Bilbury, Bucks. BY1 0ZZ Tel: 00000 00000

———————— Quality ◆ Reliability ◆ Economy ————————

Mr. T. Houseman
39 Mayflower Avenue,
Bilbury, Bucks
BY2 3AB

June 2000

Dear Mr. Houseman,

IT WILL COST YOU NOTHING TO FIND OUT

As a responsible householder you are obviously concerned that your property is well maintained. You may also be considering some improvements which will increase its value. Now, here is a chance for you to learn just how much those niggling repairs will cost, or how much you would need to invest to acquire that home extension you have been thinking about. And the service is absolutely free. The enclosed reply card offers you a convenient way to learn more.

QRE Builders has been established for over 30 years. It is a *local* company which knows your area well, and which goes to considerable lengths to live up to the company's slogan – QUALITY RELIABILITY ECONOMY.

Building, roofing, decorating, electrics, plumbing . . . QRE Builders can supply competent professional tradespeople to undertake any project you have in mind. And you'll find that prices are realistic and affordable. You can rely on us to do the job when we say we will, to the timescale we promise and the price we quote you. No excuses, no second thoughts, just a job well done.

For a limited period, we are now offering to visit you and advise you on your requirements. The service is absolutely free and includes an on-the-spot estimate of the cost with a properly itemised written quotation within a day or two. We can also offer special discounts for the over 60s.

Why not take advantage of this limited offer right away? You really do have nothing at all to lose, and a great deal to gain. No matter how large or small the job, return the reply card today. I shall look forward to hearing from you.

Yours sincerely,

Philip Tiler, Proprietor

BLACKBURY OFFICE SUPPLIES

23 Blackbury Square, Blackbury BX0 ZQ2. Tel 00000 000000

The Office Manager,
Toggle Flange Ltd.
Flange Works,
Brick Lane
Bluebury BZ2 3QP

June 2000

Dear Office Manager,

The only book you'll ever need – and it's free!

You have one of the most important jobs in your organisation. After
all, if the administration doesn't run smoothly, neither does the business.
The enclosed reply-paid card will bring you one of the most useful aids
currently available to you in doing your job. And it will cost you absolutely
nothing.

For 20 years now, Blackbury Office Supplies has been offering the most
comprehensive range of stationery, sundries and equipment available from
a local supplier. The Blackbury catalogue lists the entire range and is an
invaluable source for all those items necessary for the smooth running of an
efficient office. The enclosed leaflet gives you some idea of the quality and
variety of the products available, but only shows you a fraction of the
product range. From simple ballpoint pens to the latest fax machine,
everything you are ever likely to need features in the 120-page Blackbury
catalogue.

*As a valued catalogue holder, your requirements will receive high
priority. Receive your catalogue, consult it for the items you need,
ring us on the above number and your order will be with you within
24 hours. Guaranteed.*

Furthermore, we can arrange for a fully-trained Blackbury Representative
to call upon you at whatever intervals suit you best, so you can always be
up-to-date with what we have to offer, and can place orders with a
minimum of inconvenience to yourself.

Return the reply-paid card today. It can certainly make your job much
easier.

Yours sincerely,

Howard Penn,
Managing Director.

FUW

Fund for URBAN wildlife

101, Fritillary Lane, Loganberry, Cambs. LB0 0ZZ
Tel 00000 00000

Mr. T. Gardener,
31, Thrush Meadow,
Bluberry,
Beds
5BB 0QQ

May, 2000

Dear Mr Gardener,

Are you enjoying the sights and sounds of the wild birds returning to your garden this Spring? No? Aren't there as many as there used to be? This letter gives you an opportunity to do something about it. Use the enclosed Membership Form and reply-paid envelope to join the Fund for Urban Wildlife and you can make a very real contribution towards returning the birds, butterflies and other wildlife to our town and city gardens – just the way things used to be before pollution and other factors drove them away from us.

The Fund for Urban Wildlife is a registered charity, relying totally on its members and volunteers to continue its unique work. Your support would be invaluable to us, and your membership would also give you an immense amount of pleasure and satisfaction.

> **Join FUW and you will be able to acquire such items as nesting boxes, bird tables, organic fertilisers and much else, at a fraction of the price you would have to pay in the shops. And you will *know* that the products you purchase have been thoroughly screened to make sure that they are ideal for their purpose.**

Join FUW today. Your Membership Card will be sent by return, together with a current copy of our quarterly magazine, and as a small welcoming gifts, a set of stunning urban wildlife pictures which will delight you and your family. Please join us. We do badly need your help.

Yours sincerely

Lynn Sparrow,
Regional Director.

P.S. We urgently need volunteers for your area. Interested? Tick the box on the Membership Form for more details.

9

Using More Complex Mailings

The foregoing chapters should have given you all you need to institute a successful mailing campaign. It's like any other field of endeavour, however. Once you've become thoroughly proficient, you start to become ambitious.

So how about all these highly complicated mailings that arrive through our letterboxes these days? Is there anything in them for you?

There just might be. But don't start running before you're very confident about your ability to walk.

STARTING A COLLECTION

Sometimes it seems that mailers are getting more complex all the time. There certainly appear to be more and more pieces of paper in each envelope these days.

The proponents of these complex mailers would claim that all this complication adds interest for the recipient and therefore increases the likelihood of a reply. There must be something in that, or very large and experienced companies wouldn't keep doing it.

On the other hand, some would say that an alarming number of recipients simply get bored with the whole thing and discard the lot before reading it all.

But that doesn't mean that there aren't some bones you can pick out of such mailers to your own advantage.

Why reinvent the wheel?

This is another good reason to study all the mailings you receive, in both your private and professional capacities, and keep everything which teaches you a new trick and generally intrigues you. A great deal of thought by some highly creative and professional people goes into many of the offerings you receive, and there's no reason why you shouldn't profit from all that experience and brainpower. What sort of thing might you be looking for?

PLAYING WITH FOLDS AND SHAPES

One thing you will notice immediately when studying other people's mailings is that there are more ways of skinning a cat. All mailers do not have to be rectangular, based on an A4 format page.

It's perfectly possible to produce **virtually any size or shape mailer** you think would do a job for you. One popular device, for example, is to arrange the fold in your mailer so that the same message or illustration is visible no matter which page the reader happens to be studying.

Similarly, your printer will be happy to produce your mailer in any shape you want, even though it might mean that he has to obtain a special cutter for the job. You can even cut holes in the middle of a page in rather the same way that you will have seen in some greetings cards.

However, you do need to be very sure of what you are doing before you embark on such complexity. It is certainly not a good idea to embark on such projects unless you have a good marketing reason for doing so. Spending extra time and money producing pretty shapes and intriguing folds for their own sake is simply wasteful, and may not be effective.

But if you think you do have good reason for undertaking extra creativity in this way – go ahead. But be warned. It will cost you.

INTRODUCING GIMMICKS

Everyone likes gimmicks. An intriguing or entertaining extra element to a mailer can be useful and effective: but which comes first, the gimmick or the selling story?

It's a fact that few creative people actually sit down and say to themselves 'I will now think of a gimmick'. The creative process doesn't work that way. More frequently, an idea simply pops into the head from nowhere. Or in those cases where a gimmick is obviously needed, then experience of past campaigns might throw up an idea which can be adapted for the use in question.

The point to remember is that gimmicks must be *relevant*. It's very easy to think of a bright idea and say to oneself 'Hey! That's fun! Now how can I fit that into my campaign?'

That's a temptation which should be avoided at all costs. It can lead to distortion of the message, or even to the message being lost completely. If you doubt that, think to yourself of the number of TV commercials which you can recall for some interesting gimmick, but whose *product* you can't remember for the life of you.

The trick is to let your message lead the whole process. The easiest way to illustrate this is to quote a couple of case histories.

Hammering home the point

A large company in the power nailing field designed a complex jig system which would nail a whole wooden building together in one operation. They could see numerous applications in the building industry. The snag was that the equipment cost over £100,000.

One obvious thing for the company to do was to demonstrate their product at the Building Exhibition. But how to make sure that the people they wanted, those who could make a buying decision of that size, would come along to see it?

The decision was made to invite the managing directors of Britain's top one hundred building firms along to a special showing. The next problem was to persuade these very busy and important people to come along. The company threw the problem at their advertising agency.

This wasn't easy, and after a couple of abortive attempts, the agency passed the difficulty to a local freelance consultant who specialised in solving such unusual problems.

After a little thought he went along to a friend of his who ran a hardware store. From him he obtained a sample of a small tack hammer.

He then took it along to the agency with a swing ticket tied around its neck. The copy on the ticket gave brief details of the product and the occasion, and ended with the words:

We do hope you can join us. If not, please accept this hammer with our compliments.
BECAUSE YOU'RE GOING TO NEED IT!

There was also a tear-off reply-paid card which gave the recipient the chance to accept the invitation, but also said 'Sorry I can't come, but please send me more details'.

The hammers and tickets went out in Jiffy bags, and the operation was so successful that the company even sold the equipment off the stand.

Just a footnote. The freelance made a few extra quid on that job, courtesy of the hardware store owner, in recognition of enabling him to sell 100 tack hammers all at once.

The unignorable envelope

The second case history comes from America, where one company found, through research, that they could sell their product if only they could be sure that the prospects actually read their mailings, and there was evidence that many people didn't.

In the fullness of time, envelopes dropped on business people's desks over a wide area of the USA, bearing the following message:

DO NOT throw this envelope in the waste basket unopened.
IF YOU DO, you will break a phial of distilled water, which will spill on to a DEHYDRATED BOA CONSTRICTOR which will come out of your basket and
CRUSH YOU TO DEATH!

Well now. It would be quite impossible not to open that envelope, wouldn't it?

You see the point. Both of those stories feature gimmicks which were successful precisely because they were extremely relevant to the problem being tackled.

USING MORE COLOUR

There's no reason why you can't use more colours in your mailings if your budget can afford it and if you think that the extra expense can be justified by the extra effectiveness of your mailings.

Some products or services don't really benefit from extra colour, however, simply because they demand a sober approach. It doesn't seem likely, for example, that a will writing service needs to use lots of splashy colours.

It's also worth remembering that you can add colour to your mailings by printing on coloured paper.

PROVIDING SOMETHING TO KEEP

There is a high probability that a great many people you mail don't need your goods or services. Just at the moment. However, they may well need you in the future, perhaps in a hurry if you happen to be a plumber, for example.

You can take advantage of this situation by enclosing something with your mailer which your prospect can keep for future reference.

One time-honoured item is a small sticker, which can be mounted in a diary or at the front of a telephone directory. Your prospect then doesn't have to hunt round for the product or service you provide, and you've got a head start on your competition.

That's not the only way to go, however. Some examples:

- a credit-card sized pocket calendar

- a diary

- a list of useful telephone numbers

- a metric/imperial conversion chart

- or even, a Euro/ sterling conversion chart!

You'll think of others. Naturally, whatever you mail out for recipients to keep should have your name, address and telephone number prominently displayed.

MULTIPLE MAILING

Sometimes known as 'sequential mailing', multiple mailing is the practice of sending out a series of mailings to the same list, on the same subject, at regular intervals. This can be a series of indefinite duration, but more frequently consists of two or three mail shots, sent out at intervals of around two weeks.

This sort of operation is more often associated with the industrial and commercial market, and is usually associated with companies who run large and sophisticated mailing operations, but there can be mileage in it for the smaller organisation.

You could consider waiting a decent interval after your mailing, that is until responses have largely dried up, and then going back to the same list with, in effect, a message which says, in effect, 'Sorry we haven't heard from you. Hope you got my last letter all right. Thought I ought to give you another chance to respond to this amazing opportunity.'

If you do decide to do something like this, however, don't forget to extract the prospects who did, in fact, respond to your initial mailing. If you don't, then the people you are already in touch with could be pardoned for wondering just what sort of an inefficient outfit they're dealing with.

You'll also be familiar with the often-used newsletter system, where an organisation keeps you in touch by sending out a fairly modest journal, usually about once a quarter. This is really only another form of multiple mailing, and should adhere to all the principles you've been reading about so far – especially the one about always sending out some sort of a reply element.

The system can be quite effective, but if you do decide to adopt it then you should be sure that you are going to have enough new information to keep your newsletter fresh and lively for the foreseeable future. Conventional publishing wisdom says that you should have enough material for three such journals before you send out the first one.

Teasers

You know the sort of thing. A card arrives through your letterbox telling you on no account should you miss a letter which will be arriving for you in the next few days, because some nice gentleman is going to give you £500,000.

Somehow, it never seems to work out that way.

This system must work well for organisations with large budgets and a sophisticated mailing operation, otherwise they wouldn't keep on doing it. However, it doesn't seem at all likely that the teaser would be of much use, or very cost effective, for small companies or individuals who have to watch the pennies.

So we won't waste any more time on it.

CHECKLIST

- Start a collection of interesting mailings

- Do you need a gimmick? Can you think of one which is *relevant?*

- Would more colour be effective? Can your budget stand it?

- Have you considered something for your prospect to keep?

- Would multiple mailing be an option?

CASE STUDIES

Phil wants customers to have a permanent reminder

Phil thinks that he is in a plain, straightforward business which calls for a plain straightforward approach, therefore he doesn't think gimmicks are appropriate. He is aware, however, that people don't need building work all that often, and wants to have a presence in the households that do want building at the time they want it.

He therefore decides to include a small sticker, bearing his address details, that householders can insert in the front of their telephone directories.

Howard wants to steal a march on his competition

Howard knows that he is in a competitive business, and wants to keep the name of his company to the forefront of his market's attention.

As it happens, he has a supply of cheap ball point pens with his company's name on them. He decides to enclose one with each mailing.

Lynn decides to keep the status quo

Lynn believes that her original mailing concept will be quite adequate for her purposes. She therefore resists the temptation to complicate her mailing just at the moment, although she will keep her options open and will make further decisions dependent on the success of her initial mailing.

10

Operating Your System

You now have all the ammunition you need to launch your direct mail campaign. Now you have to fire it. Before your first letter is despatched you need to have a firm idea of how you are going to operate the system once it gets under way. Fortunately, you have one of the most experienced and sophisticated organisations in the field right at your fingertips.

That, of course, is the good old Post Office.

FINDING OUT WHAT ROYAL MAIL CAN OFFER

Royal Mail has probably been handling direct mail ever since May 1840 when the famous Penny Black was introduced as the first adhesive postage stamp in the world. No organisation knows more about the subject than they do.

Direct mail has never been more important to the Royal Mail than it is at the beginning of the 21st century. Of recent years such media as the fax machine, e-mail, electronic banking and even the mobile phone have been steadily eroding the organisation's core business. Quite simply, people, and especially business people, aren't writing as many letters as they used to. It's not surprising, therefore, that Royal Mail does all it can to encourage direct mail and offers an impressive level of help to its practitioners.

The first thing you need to do is to get in touch with your local Royal Mail business department and arrange to meet a representative. You'll need to do that, anyway, because you intend to use a reply-paid card or envelope.

The level of advice and help freely available is impressive and covers just about every topic you can think of. There is an excellent range of literature to be had, informed and freqently updated, and you'll certainly want to keep copies in your files.

It's a good idea to show your Royal Mail representative exactly what you intend to mail. He'll probably have useful suggestions to make.

Ask for his help in preparing your costings, and for his

suggestions on timing your campaign. In fact, ask him just about anything you want to know, even if it's on a subject not directly related to the Post Office.

There's just one little caveat. Royal Mail is out to get all the business it can, naturally enough, and any advice and help you may receive is coloured by that perspective. Just like any other sales rep really. Bear that in mind and you won't go far wrong.

USING FREEPOST

One of the first things you'll be discussing with Royal Mail is your use of reply-paid elements in your mailing. It's all simple enough, but you do need to talk through it, and there's a licence fee to pay.

As you know, much direct mail response is by way of the Freepost system, but the older BR (business reply) system still has its adherents.

Traditionally, Freepost was used for 'consumer' mailings direct to residential households, while BR cards were employed in the commercial sector. These lines have been blurred a little in recent years, so it's up to you, really.

Just one more thing you'll need to consider. While it's perfectly acceptable to send out your mailings by second class post, there is a decided advantage to using first class mail for your response elements. This is because it adds urgency. Your prospect will have just that little more confidence that his reply is important to you.

GETTING THE TIMING RIGHT

The actual timing of your mailings is, if not crucial, then extremely important. Sometimes, the requirement is obvious, as when you are exploiting the Christmas present buying season, for example.

However, there are less obvious things to consider.

Days of the week

When are your prospects going to receive your mailing? Traditionally, Monday is a bad day because people having to go off to work after a pleasant weekend with the family aren't at their most receptive. There's also a school of thought which says that Friday isn't a good day, either, at least in the commercial field, because everyone is trying to clear their desks before trotting off for the two-day break. This is less certain, but you might like to consider it.

The day your mailing *arrives* dictates the day it is *despatched*, of course. Talk to your Royal Mail representative and seek his advice.

Seasons

Some businesses are season sensitive, of course, and people in those activities will be able to make considered judgements about that. However, even year-round businesses are affected by the seasons of the year.

It may well be that you should, if possible, avoid the latter half of July and the whole of August. This is because, school holidays being what they are, many people are constrained to take annual vacations at that time, like it or not, and you may well miss your intended prospect entirely. In fact, it's not a bad idea to avoid school holiday periods altogether.

This syndrome doesn't affect the commercial market alone. If someone has been having a whale of a time on Ibiza, then it isn't likely that a mailing which has been lying on the doormat for over a week is going to receive the considered attention it deserves when it finally is received.

STAGGERING YOUR MAILINGS

You need to decide if you should issue all your mailings in one 'hit', or whether you should stagger them over a period.

If you are running a 'one off' mailing to a highly specialist list, consisting of just a few hundred letters, then there's probably little point in splitting them up. If, on the other hand, you see your campaign as an on-going effort, perhaps to support a sales force, then there may be a great deal of mileage in dividing your mailings into reasonably sized chunks, and issuing them at – say – weekly intervals.

The last thing a salesman wants is to be handed a large bunch of leads which he can't handle efficiently in any case, and then get no support for a month.

DECIDING FREQUENCY

How often you should mail is a matter you'll learn about through sheer experience. If this is your first properly structured mailing, then you will probably want to wait a reasonable interval before running another one.

Apart from anything else, you'll want to know how long it takes for all your responses to come in. You'll certainly need to give it at least two weeks before you can have any real idea of your response level.

Even then, you may need to be a little careful. It's not unknown for responses to a given mailing to arrive *18 months* later.

Once you have a regular mailing system effectively established, then you will be able to make a considered judgement about the frequency of future efforts.

CHECKLIST

* Contact the Post Office:

Your contact . . . .
Name . . . .
Telephone number . . . .
Fax . . . .

* Are you going to use Freepost or BR?

* On which day of the week do you wish your mailing to arrive?

* Therefore, on which day should it be mailed?

* Are you sure no seasonal factors will deplete your response level?

* Are you mailing all in one 'hit'?

* Or should you stagger your mailings?

* If so, how many should be mailed each time?

* At what intervals?

* How often do you think you should mail?

CASE STUDIES

Everyone talks to Royal Mail

Phil, Howard and Lynn all contact Royal Mail and arrange to meet a representative. After the initial meeting they make the following decisions.

Phil decides to send out all his letters at once. He considers that a Saturday arrival for his mailing would be appropriate because everyone will be at home on that morning and families can talk about his proposal more readily. He therefore arranges to mail his second class letters on Thursday.

He decides to use a Freepost reply card, and arranges that with his Royal Mail representative.

Howard has his small sales force to consider, so he decides to split his mailshot into three mailings, to be despatched on successive Mondays, ensuring a midweek arrival. By doing this, he just avoids the long summer holiday period.

He considers that a traditional BR card will serve his purposes.

Lynn also decides to split her mailings into weekly shots because she has only a small staff to handle responses. Again, she considers a midweek arrival would be appropriate, so she arranges a Monday despatch.

She arranges to use a Freepost reply-paid envelope.

11

Handling Responses

It's one thing to receive lots of lovely leads, but quite another to decide what you are going to do with them. One thing's for sure: whatever you do, you should do it *quickly*.

It's only polite to attend to enquiries without delay, but quite apart from all that, you do want your prospect to feel that his enquiry is important to you, and you certainly don't want to allow time for the enquiry to be forgotten by the person who made it.

If you are sending out literature, or some other item, as a response, then you should ensure that it is mailed on the same day that the reply card arrives back on your desk. If it is a matter of a personal follow-up, then you can, at least, make an appointment by phone within a few hours of receiving the enquiry.

But, whatever you do, eliminate all the delay from the follow-up process that you can.

DECIDING ON YOUR OWN RESPONSE

You know your own business best, so you will be able to make decisions, based on your own experience, on just what form your response to enquiries should take. Here are some suggestions:

- Should you be sending literature by post, or in the hands of a representative? 'Hallo, Mr. Jones. Nice to meet you. I was in the area, so I thought I'd drop your catalogue in personally.')

- Should you be making appointments by phone?

- Do some enquiries seem to merit more careful attention than others? You may need to keep an eye open for time-wasters.

- If you have a sales force, how are you going to arrange to get the enquiries to them without delay?

KEYING RESPONSES

Before you can find out very much about your responses you have to know which mailing they came from. That means that your reply card, coupon or whatever has to have something unique about it to enable you to recognise it quickly.

If you are only undertaking the occasional mailing, geared to individual products, for example, then you might not think that's much of a problem, but it is, you know. You may wish to refer to it months later, perhaps to compare costings, and you'll need an easy way to refer to it.

It's much safer to allocate a separate, unique reference number to each mailing, and to make sure that that number appears on the appropriate reply cards or coupons.

One favourite method is to print your reference number unobtrusively at the bottom of the coupon. As you'll probably have to reprint the card or coupon for each mailing, then that's not a problem. However if, for example, you are not sending out all your mailings at once, you may not really know which batch produced any particular response if they all bear the same reference number.

There is one handy little ploy you can use. Simply take the reply cards and guillotine off the top right-hand corners. On the next batch you repeat the exercise with the top *left*-hand corner. And so on. That gives you four batches of mailings which you can recognise immediately. The cut off corners needn't be obtrusive. A quarter-inch or so will do nicely.

That's the principle, anyway. You'll be able to think of variations on that theme, but the important thing is that all your mailings should be keyed by some means or other to enable you to make the best of your response analysis.

ANALYSING RESPONSES

There's no point in receiving large numbers of responses to your mailings unless you learn as much from them as you can. The things you want to know may vary depending on what sort of business you are in, but there are certain items of information which anyone using direct mail should be deriving from the enquiries received as the result of each mailing. They include:

The level of response

Obviously, the first thing you'll think of is just how many replies did each mailing stimulate, and was the whole exercise worthwhile.

It's easy to count the replies you receive and work out what the percentage response was. By all means do that, but it's really not quite good enough.

You will also need to know how much each reply cost you. Again, that's easy enough: simply take the costing for your mailing and divide it by the number of replies you receive. Don't be in a hurry to do that, however. You may be surprised by just how long it takes for responses to stop dribbling in.

At this point, it's worth having a word about those dreaded percentages.

Percentage returns

Most people tend to judge the success of a mailing by the number of responses received expressed as a percentage of the total number of items mailed. It's an interesting statistic, and useful when comparing the effectiveness of one mailing with that of another you've conducted in the past. But really, it's very little more than that, and you shouldn't get too hung up about it.

You might be happy to receive, let's say, a two percent return, but it's slightly terrifying to realise that that figure means that 98 out of every 100 items you've paid postage on end up in the waste basket.

But that's not the point. It's the other two which interest you.

If you receive enough business from the replies you do get to make a healthy profit on your mailing, then the whole exercise has been a success. It will, of course, depend on the unit cost of the product you are selling and a variety of other factors, but the more meaningful measure of success is the sum which tells you how much each new lead cost to obtain.

Compare that with an estimate of what that lead would have cost by other methods – cold calling by representatives, for example, and you begin to derive a useful idea of your mailing's effectiveness.

Furthermore, a successful sale as the result of a lead will probably mean repeat business, assuming the quality of your product and your before and after sales service is satisfactory.

A customer, like a dog, isn't just for Christmas.

The statistics

Here is a list of the facts you should record for the results of each mailing:

- reference number to distinguish one mailing from another

- date mailed

- date and number of responses received, day by day

- cumulative total of responses received, also day by day

- percentage response

- cost of the mailing

- unit cost per response

- notes.

Notes

That final 'notes' category largely, but not entirely, concerns the weather, believe it or not. A thoroughly filthy day, gloomy and pouring with rain, depresses everyone and makes him or her less receptive to unsolicited mailings. So does a steamingly hot and sultry day.

It isn't worth recording the weather on every day a mailing is due to arrive (although at least one major company in the direct mail field does just that), but if extremes of weather do strike on the day your mailings are due to arrive, then it's worth noting that fact. You can't actually *do* anything about it, but it might go some way towards explaining why one shot is less successful than an exactly similar one despatched a week later.

The weather isn't the only factor which can affect responses. Anything that makes people depressed is likely to depress your return. Did your local football team lose a crunch game? Has the Chancellor decreed an especially tough budget? You will know which factors affect your market most.

Unfortunately, the reverse doesn't seem to be true. There's no evidence to suggest that a spell of pleasant weather, or an especially cheerful news item, *increases* returns on mailing.

WORKING OUT THE CONVERSION FACTOR

Getting healthy returns on your mailings is one thing, but it isn't the same as converting those leads into actual business.

The conversion factor is one thing you will obviously want to know, and isn't too difficult to work out, but so many factors influence events in between receiving a response and making a sale that it's difficult to lay the blame, or the credit, on the mailing alone. Is your product good enough? Is your sales force up to scratch? How about your sales techniques?

The sheer quantity of replies is not the be-all and end-all of the matter. It can be relatively easy to increase your response rate simply by improving your offer. Try offering a free Bahamas holiday to everyone who sends back the reply card and you'd probably get a 100 per cent return, but the quality of those leads would be abysmally low, and your conversion rate close to zero.

It's a balancing act, and only experience and your knowledge of your own business will show you at what level to pitch your offer. When all is said and done, the conversion factor is the only figure, which really matters.

USING RESPONSES AS LIST BUILDERS

Finally, the people who respond to your mailings are a very valuable resource. If they've replied to you once, then they are more likely to do so again than someone who doesn't know you from Adam.

It's worth compiling a special premium mailing list of those prospects who have already responded to you. However, you might want to remove them from your main database to avoid duplication.

CHECKLIST

- Prepare a table to allow you to record your responses. It might look something like the one shown on the opposite page.

- Establish a system for following up your new leads as quickly as possible.

- Extract the names and addresses of your new prospects and start to establish a new premium mailing list

DIRECT MAIL RESPONSE ANALYSIS
Week 2 Jan to 6 Jan

Ref. No . . . . . Quantity mailed . . . . Date mailed					
Total cost					
Date responses received	2 Jan	3 Jan	4 Jan	5 Jan	6 Jan
No. responses received					
Cumulative total					
Cost/response					
Cumulative cost/response					
NOTES					

CASE STUDIES

Phil, Howard and Lynn all drew up response analysis charts.

Phil is interested in the weather

Unusually, Phil would positively welcome a spell of wet weather! He feels that heavy rain might well show householders evidence of leaks or water penetration in their property, and therefore encourage them to respond to his mailing.

Howard ensures that his reaction to responses is as fast as possible

Howard calls his small sales force into the office for a meeting on the subject of direct mail. He makes sure that each representative has ample supplies of his new catalogue to deliver to his new leads, and that they all contact his office each day for name and address details from the responses.

Lynn needs to spread the good news to her volunteers

Lynn arranges to despatch her acknowledgement of her new members, complete with their free gift, as promptly as possible. She also makes sure that her volunteers in the appropriate areas receive names and addresses of these new members for personal, local follow-up.

12

Testing! Testing!

It has been said that testing is 'the life blood of direct mail'. If you intend to make mailing an element of your marketing effort for any length of time, then you would certainly be well advised to check the efficiency of your operation on a regular basis, and also to experiment with your operation to see if you can improve it in any way.

One good reason to test things regularly is that you could well get more value from your budget. Obviously, a higher response rate will give you a lower unit cost, but there are other considerations, too.

For instance, why spend money on giving out free gifts if you find that your response rate isn't affected if you don't do so?

With a little experience you will be able to devise your own tests, but here are some pointers.

TESTING YOUR TIMING

Are you sure that you are mailing on the right day of the week? It would be perfectly simple to arrange to mail on Monday on one week, and Tuesday on the next. Alternatively, you could post half your mailings on Monday, and the rest on the following day. Either way, you should soon find out if your proposals are day-sensitive or not.

You could look at seasonal mailings in the same way. It's easy enough to decide that a Christmas mailing would be a sensible option, but just when does the Christmas buying season start in your particular markct? Again, a split mailing on successive weeks could give you useful information.

One word of warning. Such tests are not really valid unless you use identical mailing packages for each element of the test. Send out two different mailers and you are comparing apples with oranges.

VARYING YOUR COPY

One very large and internationally known company which generates most of its business by direct mail goes to great lengths to run a comprehensive programme of testing. In one such experiment, they take two identical letters and simply switch the order in which two paragraphs appear. They then arrange things so that their mailings are alternated – nos. 2, 6, 10 and 14 in one street receive version 'A' and nos. 4, 8, 12 and 16 receive version 'B'. The responses are then carefully compared.

You may not wish to go to quite those lengths, but the principle is sound. By varying your copy slightly from mailing to mailing, not only do you gain some valuable data, but you might learn more about writing, too.

CHANGING THE OFFER

You might be convinced that you are presenting your prospects with an irresistible offer, but are you sure that they see it that way? There may be another way to present your offer which, for some reason, tickles the imagination of the person reading your letter. Your product may do the job faster than the one sold by your competitor, but it's worth finding out whether that impresses your prospect more than the ability to do the job more conveniently does. In your business speed might well equate with convenience, but if you don't point that out in your mailer, then the fact might just slip by.

Another form of testing is applicable here. You can probably make a change to just one paragraph of your letter which changes the emphasis somewhat. Then send out both letters and see which works best.

CHANGING TITLES

Not the title of your letter, if any, or the title of your product, but your *own* title. Some people like to think they are dealing with the Big White Chief of an organisation, while others prefer to hear from an executive dedicated to service to customers.

Try varying your job title, now and again, and see if it makes any difference to your returns. You could easily be 'Sales Manager' and 'Customer Services Manager' as part of your brief.

It might be worth finding out which one impresses your prospects more.

USING 'BLIND' MAILERS

The 'blind' mailer is a useful device for checking whether your mailings were despatched and delivered on time, and whether they arrived at their destinations in good condition.

The system is quite simple: it consists of adding two or three addresses to your mailing list which belong to members of your staff or acquaintances who have nothing to do with the operation at all, and who have been warned to expect them on the given date. You could even use your own private address for the purpose, but it makes sense to spread your blind mailers widely over your designated mailing area.

Obviously, the first thing you will be watching is whether your mailers arrived when they should have done. However, it's also a good idea to open them carefully and check that they contain all the items you intended, that they were folded and inserted tidily, and that your package presents the attractive, professional look for which you were aiming.

ASK!

Don't be afraid to ask people on your list what they thought of your mailing. You could seek information from people who respond and also from people who don't.

In the first case you could enquire just what factor encouraged your prospect to respond, and in the second, was there anything wrong with the product, or did the mailing simply not enthuse them?

It's all good grist to the mill of future mailings.

COMPARING WITH OTHER FORMS OF PROMOTION

It's a truism to state that a combination of direct mail and press advertising is more effective than either medium used alone. That may or may not be true in your case, but you can always try to find out by taking a local press or trade press ad scheduled to appear at the same time that some of your mailers burst upon a startled world. You can then compare responses between the two mailings.

If you don't want to go to that extra expense, then try issuing a press release at the appropriate time.

Be meticulous with your records

We probably don't have to say this, but you do need to be meticulous and up-to-date about your record keeping if your testing is to mean much. That's so obvious that it doesn't need expanding, but it's only right to mention it here.

Whatever you do – TEST!

The foregoing give you some ideas about how to test the efficiency and effectiveness of your direct mail operations. They are not the only things you might try, of course, and you'll find some other suggestions in the checklist below. Over to you!

CHECKLIST

- Run tests to see if you are:
  - mailing on the best day
  - using seasonal factors to the most effective extent
  - presenting your copy in the best order
  - making the best offer
  - using the most effective job title below your signature.

- Organise blind mailers.

- Arrange to ask some recipients about your mailing.

- Take an ad or issue a press release to coincide with some of your mailings.

Some more suggestions for testing

Try varying:

- the colour of the paper your letters are printed on

- the colour of the material your reply cards or envelopes are printed on

- the size of the typeface in your letter

- the typeface itself

- the piece of literature (if any) you are enclosing with your letter
- your signature ('J W Smith' or the friendlier 'John Smith')
- . . . in fact, vary anything you think worth trying.

CASE STUDIES

Phil wonders about his timing
Although Phil has a perfectly good reason for timing his mailings to arrive on a Saturday, he does wonder if a weekend delivery is really a good idea. He decides to arrange for one-third of his letters to be posted a day earlier.

Howard varies his literature
Howard has a wide range of sales literature available to him. He therefore arranges to enclose three different brochures in three separate parts of his mailing.

Lynn aranges blind mailings
Lynn has volunteers in widely scattered parts of her region. She writes to six of them, telling them to expect a mailing similar to the one enclosed with her letter, and asks them to return the mailing to her with a note of thc datc of arrival. She remembers, at the last moment, to add these six addresses to her mailing list!

Not only does this give her a useful check on the efficiency of her operation, but she also feels that this is a useful way for her to keep volunteers involved.

13

Going on from Here

MEASURING YOUR SUCCESS

When you've completed your first direct mail campaign and are fairly confident that the vast majority of your responses have arrived and are in the process of being followed up, then you'll be able to have a good think about how successful you've been.

One of the great strengths of the medium is that it gives you a firm, hard measure of success. You know how many responses you've received and how much each one has cost you. Later on you'll be able to assess your conversion rate and so estimate how much actual business your campaign has generated for you.

So where do you go from here?

If you have achieved all the success you wanted, then there would appear to be no problem. On the other hand, if you have not received the level of response you expected, then the tendency is for discouragement to set in.

Don't let that happen. Almost anything can be sold by direct mail, if you set about it properly. An initial disappointment simply means that you haven't found the right formula yet. Any scientist will tell you that there's no such thing as a failed experiment: just a negative result which can teach you something.

Even very large organisations which have been generating most of their sales by direct mail for decades have their failures on occasion, and there is also the thought that Murphy's Law may have struck on your first foray into the medium, depressing responses through some factor which is the fault of neither you nor your campaign.

'Keep on keeping on' as the saying goes. Don't dismiss the whole field because of one disappointment; rather, say to yourself, 'What can I learn from this?'

However, the likelihood is that your first properly structured campaign may not have been a world-rocking triumph, but won't have been an abject failure. So now you need to maximise your strengths, and eliminate your weaknesses.

REFINING YOUR BUDGET

The first thing you can do is take a hard-eyed look at your costs and see if there are ways in which you can make your budget work for you more efficiently. There may be expenses you hadn't expected. There may be areas where, knowing what you know now, some expenditure could have been avoided altogether. Could your design and print have been produced more economically, or to higher standards of quality for the same money?

Are you sure that your control of expenditure was as ironclad as it could be?

Be as hard-nosed as you can. Ask yourself, 'How could I explain this to my bank manager?'

MORE OR MORE EXPENSIVE?

It doesn't matter how successful your campaign has been, you'll always be striving for a greater number of responses next time round. It could be that the answer is simply to increase the size of your mailing list, send out more packages, and get more replies that way.

Some people don't have that option, however. They may have their potential market pretty well saturated to start with. There is a finite number of people in any given trade in any area, and if you've mailed them all, then there isn't much you can do about it, other than spread your wings into a larger geographical region. If you can do that – well and good, but there may be constraints on just how far from your headquarters you can operate effectively.

In that case, your mailers have to attract a higher level of response if they are to generate more business. Perhaps you need to spend more on each one.

This isn't a subject on which you can easily be advised here. You are going to have to decide the question 'more or more expensive' for yourself on the basis of the considerable amount of information you have derived from your initial campaign.

This could be the point at which you call in the professionals, perhaps by seeking advice from a local direct mail agency. On the other hand, it might not. You may well be able to make your own decisions from your existing data. After all, you're a direct mail professional yourself now, aren't you?

LOOKING AT YOUR FOLLOW-UP

The other thing to look at is your conversion rate. Are you sure that you derived as much business as you might have done from your responses?

- Were they followed up quickly enough?

- Did you make the best possible sales pitch?

- Was your sales force properly briefed?

It may be that your mailing did its job, but that its success could have been maximised subsequently.

DON'T PULL THE TRIGGER QUIETLY!

Wherever you go from here, do be sure to make as much noise about it as you can. Make your company *visible* perhaps by attending local shows, or whatever, sponsoring local events, issuing press releases, holding an open day – whatever it takes.

The aim is for a recipient of your mailing to say to himself 'Ah yes! I've heard of these people. Perhaps I should get in touch.'

No hard and fast rules

As was stated right from the outset, there aren't any hard and fast rules in the direct mail business, just proven techniques which work most of the time.

That being so, if you find evidence which seems to indicate that you should do something which runs counter to advice given here, then – as long as you're sure – go right ahead.

And the very best of luck in all your endeavours.

Appendix 1
Post Office Services

MAILSORT

A service which offers discounts on postage for mailings of at least 4,000 identical letters or 1,000 identical packages. To qualify, mail must be sorted into postcode districts before delivery to the Post Office in bundles. Discounts can be as high as 32 percent. Mailsort options are as follows:

- Mailsort 1
  Targeted for delivery on the next working day.

- Mailsort 2
  Targeted for delivery with three working days.

- Mailsort 3
  Targeted for delivery within seven working days.

Mailsort Light

A service which offers extra discounts for preceding your mail mailing with a 'teaser', or following up with a reminder.

Presstream

A similar service to mailsort designed to provide a nationwide distribution service for periodicals, magazines and newsletters.

Response Services

Business Reply and Freepost systems allow you to enclose reply-paid cards and envelopes with your mailings. A small premium is payable on all returned items, and the services require a Response Services Licence and a nominal annual fee.

Go Direct

A service specifically designed to assist the small business. The membership package includes a six-day-a-week telephone helpline, a range of fact sheets, a quarterly bulletin, an annual case history booklet and an annual *Go Directory* of useful contacts and topics.

Recommended for small businesses using direct mail on a 'do it yourself' basis.

Door to Door
The service which delivers unaddressed mail. Can be utilised on a local, regional or national level. Ensures delivery by morning post.

Postcode products
The Postcode Address File (PAF) is the most complete and up-to-date address database in the UK, containing some 25 million addresses.

Royal Mail Sales Centres
This is your first point of contact with the Royal Mail for advice and help on direct mail matters. The central telephone number, which connects you to your local centre, is 0345 950950, during normal business hours.

Appendix 2
Using an Agency

All being well, the time will come when you will consider using the services of a specialist **direct mail agency** to handle your operation for you. There will probably be a fairly wide choice of such organisations within striking distance, so the first question is, which one to pick?

CHOOSING AN AGENCY

First and foremost, make sure you select a specialist. Don't be tempted to give your business to a general advertising agency, because however good they are at what they do, they won't know as much about the subject as the genuine specialist does. In fact, they might even sub-contract some aspects of your account to a specialist anyway.

Here are some things to look for:

Track record
Any agency will be clamouring to show you the work they've done for other people. Fair enough: you'll want to see it, but always remember that the question isn't 'what have you done for other companies?' it's 'what can you do for me?'

In any case, you will want to see the agency's client list. It only makes sense to give preference to an outfit that is experienced in working in similar fields to your own, but watch out for names of companies who are in competition with you.

There are rules about this sort of thing. No reputable agency will take you on if there is likely to be a conflict of interest with another of their clients, but from their point of view, it may not be immediately obvious that such a conflict might arise. The rule is – if in doubt, don't use them.

Lists

No agency is any better than the lists they provide. You will want to know:

- How they will set about compiling lists for your particular project.

- Do they already have such lists, and if not, from where will they obtain them?

- That the lists they use are clean and maintained regularly.

It's a good idea not to be too forthcoming about your own lists and how you obtained them. Let them come up with those ideas, and see if they gel with your own. Secondly, your list might just be a saleable item!

People

Some business relationships can operate perfectly well on an adversarial basis – you don't have to like a chap to be able to work with him. This field, however, is emphatically not one of them. You need to be comfortable with the people who will be working on your account.

One of the first things an agency will do is to introduce you to an **account executive** who will be your primary point of contact, and responsible for all aspects of your account. (Titles may vary, but 'account executive' is what he or she is.)

Fine. If you like the character concerned, all well and good. But it's wise to go a little further than that. You might ask to meet the people who will be working on your account, preferably in their own professional environment.

You might be in for the odd surprise. Creative people often don't fit into the traditional business mould, so don't expect them to. One of the best designers in Cheltenham, which is a very busy centre for the promotional trades, had a piano in his office for years.

The whole point is that you must be able to get on the same wavelength as your agency people. If you aren't then it's unlikely that they will produce work that you like, or that can do the best job for you.

Perhaps the best single piece of advice would be 'trust your gut feel'.

Appendix 3
Using Freelances

If you do not, as yet, want to go as far as employing a direct mail agency, then a good halfway house is to venture into the freelance market. In fact, you may want to do that in any case, because it isn't a good idea to entrust the design of your material to your printer.

There are plenty of self-employed commercial artists about and they come in all shapes and sizes, covering all aspects of the graphic professions. It's a hard, highly competitive business to be in, seriously overcrowded in most areas, and consequently, every designer you talk to will assure you that you won't get a better job from anyone.

You do, of course, need to be sure that you have the right person for the job, and the first thing to do is take a look at the designer's specimen portfolio. That should show you if he or she has a style appropriate to your business, and, equally important, how experienced the designer is.

Freelance copywriters are not so thick on the ground, but any designer, or possibly printer, you use will know someone appropriate for your purposes. Don't make the mistake of confusing copywriters with journalists. They are two entirely different disciplines, working to quite dissimilar parameters.

Again, it's important to be comfortable with the people you choose.

One thing you positively must do is find out just how much your freelance is going to charge you. Better still, tell them what your budget is before you start, and make it clear that you are not going to deviate from it.

Further Reading

Books about direct mail are readily available, and there are quite a few of them. You will certainly acquire Royal Mail's excellent *Direct Mail Guide* along the way, and other books you might like to try include Iain Maitland's *How to Plan Direct Mail* and *Do it Yourself Advertising: How to Produce Direct Mail* by Fred Hahn. Your local library will probably have copies of these and others.

As an aid to writing your own material, *The Concise Oxford English Dictionary*, or a similar publication is recommended, as is *Fowler's Modern English Usage*. *Roget's Thesaurus* is a valuable book for helping you to find a turn of phrase.

You will find a small collection of general reference books useful to help you get ideas about your mailing efforts, and stimulate the creative process generally. *The Oxford Dictionary of Quotations* is found on many copywriters' shelves for this purpose, while *Brewer's Dictionary of Phrase and Fable* offers an unrivalled collection of thought-provoking facts and oddities.

Glossary

AIDA. A mnemonic designed to assist in the structure of a direct mail letter. The acronym denotes **Attract, Interest, Direct, Action.**

Blind mailers. Mailers sent out as part of a mailing specifically to check on the promptness of a mailing's delivery, and the condition in which it arrives.

BR Cards (envelopes). Royal Mail's reply-paid service, intended for use with commercial rather than consumer mailings. BR is an acronym for business reply. See Freepost.

Cleaning. The process of keeping mailing lists up to date by removing redundant addresses or duplication.

Conversion rate. The figure which indicates how much actual business resulted from a particular mailing.

Drop. See hit.

Freepost. Royal Mail's reply-paid service intended for use with consumer rather than commercial mailings. See BR Cards.

Hit. A colloquial term indicating a quantity of mailings arriving at prospects' addresses on the same day. Also known as a 'drop'.

Keying. The important practice of indicating which particular mailing stimulated an individual response by printing a reference on the reply card or envelope.

Mailer. The individual package, including envelope, reply card, letter and whatever additional items thought desirable sent out in quantity as part of a mailing.

Mailing. A quantity of mailers posted to a group of prospects simultaneously.

Multiple mailing. A series of mailings sent to an identical mailing list at intervals. Sometimes known as sequential mailing.

Response. A reply received as a result of a mailing.

Self-liquidator. A special offer priced at a level which liquidates the cost of the item under offer to the seller and no more. The best bargains may well come from the vendor's own product range.

Sequential mailing. See multiple mailing.

Teaser. An advance mailer sent to warn recipients of a main mailing to follow later.

Tone of voice. The manner in which a recipient is addressed by the mailer. Should the language used be formal, colloquial or businesslike? The mode of address is echoed in the design and production of the material itself.

UTGP. An acronym which stands for 'Understand the Guy's Problem'. In other words, put yourself in your prospect's place and imagine what he, or she, really wants from you. The standpoint from which all direct mail letters should be written.

Widget. A 'value-added' device, such as a free gift or self-liquidator, designed to increase the level of response.

Index